AGINCOURT

The monument to those of both armies who fell at Agincourt. (Peter Hoskins)

AGINCOURT
1415

*A Tourist's Guide to the Campaign
by Car, by Bike and on Foot*

Peter Hoskins
with Anne Curry

Pen & Sword
MILITARY

First published in Great Britain in 2014 by
PEN & SWORD MILITARY
an imprint of
Pen & Sword Books Ltd
47 Church Street
Barnsley
South Yorkshire
S70 2AS

ISBN 978 1 78383 157 9

A CIP catalogue record for this book is
available from the British Library.

Typeset in Palatino and Optima by
CHIC GRAPHICS

Printed in India by Replika Press Pvt. Ltd.

Pen & Sword Books Ltd incorporates the imprints of
Pen & Sword Archaeology, Atlas, Aviation, Battleground, Discovery,
Family History, History, Maritime, Military, Naval, Politics, Railways,
Select, Social History, Transport, True Crime, and Claymore Press,
Frontline Books, Leo Cooper, Praetorian Press, Remember When,
Seaforth Publishing and Wharncliffe.

For a complete list of Pen & Sword titles please contact
PEN & SWORD BOOKS LTD
47 Church Street, Barnsley, South Yorkshire, S70 2AS, England
E-mail: enquiries@pen-and-sword.co.uk
Website: www.pen-and-sword.co.uk

CONTENTS

PREFACE

The origins of this guide lie in my project, which I started in 2005, to follow on foot the campaigns of the Black Prince leading to his victory over King John II of France at the Battle of Poitiers in 1356. The aim was to bring a fresh look to the campaigns of 1355 and 1356 by supplementing more conventional historical research with exploration on the ground.

Some readers found the book that followed, *In the Steps of the Black Prince, The Road to Poitiers 1355–1356*, useful and interesting when touring near the routes of the Black Prince's campaigns, even though it lacked both detailed information on routes and practical information for tourists. Although it was not intended as a guide book, it was evident that the story and the places that featured in *In the Steps of the Black Prince* provided the elements for interesting holidays or excursions for those with an interest in history.

With the approach of the 600th anniversary of the Battle of Agincourt it seemed, based on my experience with *In the Steps of the Black Prince*, that there was room for a book specifically written to help the historical tourist follow the campaign. This book takes the tourist from the likely landing place for Henry V and his army close to modern Le Havre through the battlefield near the village of Agincourt to Calais, where Henry embarked for England.

The guide tells the story of the campaign, drawing on my experience walking the route of the English march. For the history I have drawn extensively on Anne Curry's work, including her books *Agincourt, A New History*, and *The Battle of Agincourt: Sources and Interpretations*, as well as local histories. This book is a guide book following Henry V's route provided by Anne Curry in *Agincourt, A New History*. It is not intended to be an analytical history of the campaign, and it does not, therefore, either discuss in depth some of the uncertainties associated with the battle and Henry's march, or attempt to analyse and interpret the varying accounts in the primary sources. Where there is such uncertainty

I have opted for what seems to me to be the most probable interpretation. The choices are mine.

Those who would like authoritative detail and analysis can do no better than read Anne Curry's books. In her *The Battle of Agincourt, Sources and Interpretation* she reproduces a wide range of primary sources and describes their importance and interest in relation to the campaign. In *Agincourt, A New History* she brings the sources together in detailed discussion and analysis of the sometimes conflicting sources, and gives a lively and absorbing account of the siege of Harfleur, the onward march and the battle.

Peter Hoskins

ACKNOWLEDGEMENTS

I am particularly grateful to Anne Curry for her contribution to this book. When I first conceived the idea for a guide for tourists, I appreciated that it would be impossible to write a useful guide without drawing extensively on her body of work. Such is the extent of her expertise that I could not see any way forward without her collaboration. I was, therefore, delighted when she offered to allow me to draw on her research and also to advise on the text. She has given a good deal of her time and patience to advising me and I cannot thank her enough for her guidance.

I am also grateful to my companions John Griffin, Martin Hoskins and Richard Kinnear, who patiently followed parts of the route with me. John, Martin and Andrew Vallance also read an early draft, and as always gave particularly valuable advice. Thanks are also due to Christophe Gilliot, director of the Centre Historique Médiéval d'Azincourt, for devoting an afternoon to showing me around and for the wealth of information he imparted that I could not have found without him, not least the results of his research on the Azincourt family. My thanks also to those who have allowed me to use their photographs and illustrations: Frédéric Louessard, Paul Hitchen, George Griffin, Chris Dawson and Richard Kinnear. Finally, and by no means least, thanks to Scott Hall for the time and skill he has devoted to drawing the maps and plans.

ADVICE FOR TOURISTS

Introduction

This guide has been written primarily with the motorist in mind, but with additional information for those who want to follow the routes either on foot or on a touring bicycle. The guide is divided into five tours following the itinerary of Henry V and his army from the landing near modern Le Havre, through the battlefield at Agincourt, or Azincourt as it is known to the French, to Calais where the army embarked for home. Two tours are local to the scene of events: the first dealing with the landings and the siege of Harfleur and the fifth covering the battlefield. A half-day visit will be sufficient for a visit to the area of the landings and the siege, and a similar period will allow ample time to see the battlefield and the museum in the village of Agincourt. The other three tours can each be covered in a day or so by car. Three or four days would be comfortable for a cyclist, and the walker will need to allow about a week. Walking the entire route would require about three weeks.

How to Get There and Back by Public Transport

The tours start and finish at towns of sufficient size to provide a selection of accommodation. The nearest airports for each tour are given, and with the walker and cyclist in mind there is information on rail access to the start and end of each tour. Information is also given on intermediate towns with access by public transport to enable walkers and cyclists to tailor tours to meet time available or particular interests.

The French railways, *SNCF*, have an extensive network. They also run co-ordinated bus, *autocar* or *car*, services as replacements for defunct lines to link some rail services. The website for planning a journey is www.voyages-sncf.com. An English language version, www.voyages-sncf.co.uk, will take you to Rail Europe, www.raileurope.co.uk. These sites generally give you all the information you need for the route. However, the network is organized regionally and full timetables, details on station services and locations, and route maps are given on regional websites. Start on www.ter-sncf.com and then go to the appropriate region: Haute-Normandie, Picardie and Nord-Pas-de-Calais.

Eurolines, www.eurolines.fr, operate a number of long-distance bus routes in France. However, there is no equivalent to National Express in the UK, and finding details of local bus services can be time consuming. A good starting point will often be the website for the prefecture of the *département* in question. Some towns also have websites which give information about bus and coach services. Many rural bus services are geared to getting people to and from work and children to and from school, so there are often services early in the morning, around midday and in the evening, with little or nothing in the way of services in between.

For those walkers and cyclists travelling to and from the tours by car, parking is available at *SNCF* stations at the start and finish of each route and at intermediate points. Outside of major towns parking at stations is generally free. In addition, it is usually possible to find other parking free of charge in small towns and villages. However, some car parks double as market-places, and when parking it is advisable to check that there is not a parking prohibition on market days. This will normally be indicated on a sign nearby. French railways are relatively bicycle-friendly, and it is usually possible to take a bicycle, *vélo*, on the train: www.velo.SNCF.com. Cyclists should check before planning a tour, but there is not normally a charge for taking cycles on regional trains, *TER*. Similarly, carriage on some Intercity trains, *IC*, is free, but sometimes a reservation is required and in that case a charge is levied. Capacity on high-speed trains, *TGV*, is limited, reservation is mandatory and invariably a charge will be made. Carriages in which bicycles can be loaded are generally marked with a large bicycle symbol on the window, and in some trains easy-to-use hanging racks are provided. Bicycles cannot generally be taken on buses, but some buses operated by *SNCF* do carry cycles. Information on cycle carriage on *SNCF*-operated buses can be found on the route timetable, *fiche horaire*, on regional websites, and the *SNCF* journey planner on the main French site, www.voyages-SNCF.com, also indicates services on which bicycles can be carried with standard symbols. This site also indicates when disabled access is available on a service.

Where to Stay

In view of the dynamic nature of the accommodation market, and differing personal preferences for accommodation and daily travelling distances, I have not given specific information on accommodation. However, there is a wide range of up-to-date information available on the Internet with a number of excellent websites to help in the search for accommodation. For bed and breakfast *Gîtes de France*, www.gites-de-france.com, *Clévacances*, www.clevacances.com, and *Airbnb*, www.airbnb.com, are good starting points. *Logis*, www.logishotels.com, provides information on a wide range of independent hotels. All these websites have an interactive map search facility with an option for use in English, and *Gîtes de France*, *Clévacances* and *Logis* all publish printed guides. Yellow Pages, *Pages Jaunes*, www.pagesjaunes.fr, can also be useful and results are shown on maps. Tourist offices, *office* or *bureau de tourisme*, and town websites also often give details of accommodation, *hébergement*. A list of the more important tourist offices is given for each tour.

Finding accommodation can be particularly problematic for the walker, who cannot deviate significant distances from the route to find a bed and breakfast or hotel. If the tourist websites do not bring results, then a general Internet search for *chambre d'hôte* at the planned destination may do so. All *chambres d'hôte* are required to register with their local *mairie*, the municipal office in each town or village, *commune*. A call to the *mairie*, which can be found through *Pages Jaunes*, may throw up something not available through other sources. This may need some persistence, since in small villages the *mairie* will often not be open throughout the week. Another avenue is to post a notice on either the Normandy or Picardy & Nord-Pas-de-Calais regional websites of Anglo Info France, a network for expatriates: http://france.angloinfo.com.

Municipal and private campsites are numerous in France, but many have a short season. Town and tourist office websites are again useful sources of information for campers. A further source is: www.camping france.com/UK/. Camping in the wild, *camping sauvage*, may seem attractive in a large country such as France. However, there are restrictions on camping away from established sites, particularly in forests and national or regional natural parks. Details on regulations and some recommended sites can be found at http://le-camping-sauvage.fr.

A word of warning: many bed and breakfast businesses are a secondary form of income for a single proprietor. Thus the owner may be away at work when you arrive. Similarly, some small hotels may not be open in the afternoon, and you can find yourself in the disconcerting situation of arriving tired at the end of the day to find your accommodation locked and without signs of life. This is bad enough in a car or on a bicycle, but on foot and in the depths of the country it can be very dispiriting. It is advisable to check hotel opening hours and to notify your hotel or bed and breakfast hosts of your expected arrival time. Bed and breakfasts very rarely take credit cards, and payment will have to be made in cash or by a cheque drawn on a French bank. Similarly, small hotels sometimes do not take cards.

Where to Eat
Availability of food and drink can be problematic on foot, both at your destination and en-route. Bed and breakfasts will often provide an evening meal, *table d'hôte*, but this needs to be confirmed and booked in advance. Those in towns or villages where there are restaurants and cafés are less likely to cater for evening meals. If you are on foot and your chosen bed and breakfast does not offer evening meals, then it is always worth asking if an exception can be made – sometimes your host will provide a cold plate, *collation*, on request. Some bed and breakfasts have kitchenette areas.

Opening days and times are among the mysteries of rural and small town France. Many hotels, restaurants and bars are family run and do not open throughout the week. There is no obvious rule, with some closing when you would least expect it on Friday or Saturday evening. If you are not eating at your bed and breakfast or hotel it is worth a check beforehand that there is somewhere open. As with accommodation, town and tourist office websites can be useful. Look for where to eat, *où manger*, or *restauration*. *Pages Jaunes*, www.pages jaunes.fr, will often reveal cafés or restaurants not listed elsewhere. Search for *bars, cafés, restaurants* or *brasseries*.

The tours pass through parts of rural France with a low population density, where cafés and shops are few and far between. Also, for those of us used to shopping seven days a week, rural France can be something of a culture shock, with shops often closed at midday, rarely being open on Sunday, except bakers, and often closed on Monday. Unfortunately the size of a settlement on the map is not a reliable guide to facilities available. If walking or cycling it is advisable to carry a reserve of sufficient food for a couple of lunches. Bakers often sell sandwiches, and will also sell you half a French stick, *baguette,* if you do not want a full loaf. They generally open early in the morning and close late in the evening, but they can be closed for a protracted period around midday. If you think bread may be difficult to come by and you are staying in a bed and breakfast, it is worth calling ahead and asking your host to get you some for the next day.

One aspect of French cafés or bars which is very different from the situation in the UK is that, if they do not serve meals, they are very happy for you to bring your own food. Indeed, they will often direct you to a shop where you can buy a snack or a sandwich to bring back into the bar.

Routes

There is not the space in this volume to provide the driver, walker or cyclist with comprehensive guidance and large-scale maps for a total distance of over 500km. However, descriptions of the routes by car in the tours give sufficient information to enable the motorist to follow routes easily using a road atlas. Of course, a satellite navigation system will make life even easier. The routes by car described in the tours generally use numbered roads, *routes nationales* with an N prefix, and *routes départementales* with a D prefix but avoid motorways, *autoroutes.* Minor, unnumbered roads are occasionally suggested.

Routes on foot for each tour are described in sufficient detail to allow the walker to find the route easily using 1:25,000 scale maps (*TOP 25 et Série Bleu*) published by the *Institut National de l'Information Géographique et Forestière (IGN).* Walking routes are either shorter or, more frequently, quieter and more pleasant than the routes by car. They do not, other than for short distances where it is unavoidable, use N roads. They often follow D roads and minor unnumbered country roads, and use tracks and footpaths where possible. Many D roads are very quiet, but others can be quite busy, and the prefix to the road number can be misleading. Some busy roads previously classified as N have been re-classified as D simply to allow central government to delegate funding responsibility to the *départements.*

The routes for cyclists are, where possible, the same as those for walkers. Variations for cyclists from the routes on foot are given only where the walking routes may be unsuitable for cycling. A road atlas may suffice for cyclists if they are happy to keep to numbered roads.

However, the cyclist who wishes to get away from main roads will require more detailed maps. The *IGN* publishes a selection of maps at 1:100,000 (*Cartes Tourisme et Découverte: TOP 100*) and 1:50,000 (*Série Orange*) as well as the 1:25,000 (*Série Bleu*).

Maps published by the *IGN* are listed for each tour and can be obtained from www.ign.fr or suppliers in the United Kingdom such as Stanford Travel: http://travel.stanfords.co.uk. When choosing maps for walking or cycling it should be borne in mind that some of the *Série Orange* 1:50,000 scale maps have not been updated for more than fifteen years. Also, some of this series may not be obtainable since the *IGN* is not replacing stocks as they become exhausted.

I have not divided walking and cycling routes into daily sections, since everyone will have their own preferences for pace and distance. The route descriptions were accurate at the time of writing, but things do change as new roads are constructed and paths come and go. Walkers and cyclists should check that they have the latest edition of maps and be prepared to adapt to changes when they are on tour.

Walking and Cycling in France

A marked difference between the UK and France for walkers and cyclists is that there are no rights of way on paths in the sense that we understand them in Great Britain. In addition, tracks come and go. Just because a track is on the map does not mean it is on the ground, and just because a track is on the ground does not mean it is on the map. Sometimes what looks like a good track or minor road on the map just disappears into a field, or a house has been built across it surrounded by a long impenetrable fence. I have on occasion struck off across fields on a compass bearing to intercept a road rather than retrace my steps. Fortunately, French farmers are generally relaxed about property rights and seem to think nothing of a walker trudging across their land in search of the path, and of course the French are generally very well disposed towards cyclists.

France is blessed with an extensive network of way-marked footpaths. Many of these are organized locally, but others come under the auspices of the French walking association *Fédération Française de la Randonnée*: www.ffrandonnee.fr. National long-distance paths are known as *Sentiers de Grande Randonée*, and given a number prefixed *GR* (e.g. *GR353*); they are way-marked in red and white. Horizontal red and white bars mark the route, a red and white cross means 'not this way', and red and white arrows set at right angles indicate turns. Regional routes are known as *Sentiers de Grande Randonnée du Pays (GRP)*. These routes are way-marked in a similar way in red and yellow. *GR* and *GRP* paths are usually marked on recent editions of 1:25,000 maps. Local routes which are generally of short distance and aimed more at the rambler out for the day are known as *Sentiers de Promenade et Randonnée (PR)*; they are way-marked in yellow. On occasions the tours in the guide follow designated paths for short distances and the way marking can be useful.

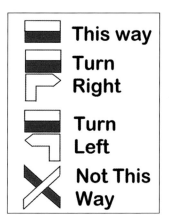

Conventional footpath signs: red and white for long-distance paths (GR) and red and yellow for regional paths (GRP), but frequently used in different colours for other paths.

Many forests in France are open to the public and provide long pleasant walks, often in ancient oak woods, but occasionally forest areas are private and are fenced off for hunting – *chasse privé* or *chasse gardé*. Furthermore, hunting in public areas in France, in the sense of shooting of deer and boar, *sanglier*, with rifles, is widespread in the hunting season. The dates for the hunting season vary from region to region, but typically the season runs from late August or early September to the beginning of March. The season can be longer in fenced-off parks or forests. In public areas roads where hunting is in progress will be marked with signs such as *chasse en cours*. The hunters themselves will be wearing fluorescent jackets and will take every precaution to respect walkers, but it would be foolhardy to go off the main tracks in woods where hunting is under way. Apart from the risks due to the hunting itself, crossing the path of a boar being pursued by hounds is not to be recommended. In normal circumstances these magnificent beasts are most unlikely to pose a threat, but they are wild animals and they can be aggressive either to defend their young or if they feel threatened. Boar are very numerous in France, and hunting is regulated to maintain a stable population: around half a million boar are killed every year to achieve this. Despite this, I have not seen boar during my walks of more than 3,000km in France, although I have often seen signs of their presence.

As a final point, I advise walkers to carry a compass. This may seem unnecessary for this kind of walking, but I have frequently found it useful to resolve a route ambiguity, to walk where a track has disappeared and even to find the way out of a town!

Safety

The routes described in this guide are neither remote nor in the 'big outdoors'. Nonetheless, some sections of the walks are on paths away from roads or in forests that are used infrequently. In addition, mobile telephone coverage is by no means comprehensive. A minor accident in such circumstances can become hazardous, and it is prudent to take some basic safety precautions. I always carry a survival bag and a whistle to attract attention. I also always leave an itinerary with someone, giving start and stop points and accommodation planned for each day. If I am walking alone, I invariably telephone each evening the person who holds the itinerary to confirm my safe arrival.

France is less densely populated than the United Kingdom, and cycling and walking can be a great pleasure. Nevertheless, walking or cycling on roads is not without risk and some simple precautions should be taken. The French highway code, *Code de la Route*, requires pedestrians to use footpaths alongside the roads when provided rather than walking on the road. Where there are no paths, then the pedestrian must walk on the left-hand side of the road unless this presents a hazard to them. Pedestrians and cyclists are also strongly advised to wear high-visibility clothing or tabards; this is particularly important in poor visibility. Other than on the quietest of roads walkers are also well advised to walk in single file.

What Happened

There is an introductory chapter, Henry V and the Hundred Years War, to put the story of the Agincourt campaign within its historical context. Each tour also has a description of events relevant to the route followed.

What to See

The tours go through areas which suffered extensive damage during the First and Second World Wars. In the First World War some villages were totally obliterated, and had to be rebuilt completely. Much of the rich medieval heritage of this part of France was destroyed, but some survived and some was painstakingly restored. For each tour places to visit are recommended and numbered in the narrative of events, the route descriptions and on the maps. These places are those of historical interest linked to the story of the campaign and generally have buildings that at least have elements which have either survived from the time of Henry's Agincourt adventure or have been faithfully restored. Directions to places of interest away from the main route are given for the motorist, but the walking and cycling tours only take in the principal places along the main route. GPS co-ordinates are given for places to visit. The co-ordinates are in decimal form, but there are numerous conversion websites available if degrees, minutes and seconds of latitude and longitude are preferred.

HENRY V AND THE HUNDRED YEARS WAR

Henry V's great victory at the Battle of Agincourt holds a special place in English consciousness, particularly through Shakespeare's play *Henry V*. The play covers a wide scope including the siege of Harfleur, the battle and the betrothal of Catherine de Valois, daughter of Charles VI of France, to Henry V. However, it is the battle that stands out to many as central to the play and it is often viewed in isolation from the broader history of the Hundred Years War. So how do Henry V's campaign in France, his victory at Agincourt in 1415 and his subsequent achievements fit within the Hundred Years War as a whole?

Causes of the Hundred Years War

When Henry V came to the throne in 1413 the two underlying causes of the war, which had started in 1337, remained central to the relations between England and France: the homage claimed by the French kings from the kings of England for their lands in France and the English claim to the throne of France.

The anomaly whereby English kings owed homage to the kings of France can be traced back to William the Conqueror, who was both King William I of England and Duke of Normandy. The situation was exacerbated when Henry II came to the throne in 1154. He had acquired extensive lands in south-western France through his marriage to Eleanor of Aquitaine. Thus, he and subsequent English kings ruled the Duchy of Aquitaine centred on the city of Bordeaux. The status of Aquitaine was a persistent cause of dispute between the kings of England and France over the years, with the kings of France demanding homage from the English kings who proclaimed their right to full sovereignty. In the years immediately preceding the Hundred Years War there were protracted diplomatic wrangles between Edward III and Philip VI. Matters came to a head in 1337 with a dispute over the extradition from England of a French exile, Robert of Artois, a one-time adviser to Philip. Philip declared Edward's Duchy of Aquitaine forfeit, and with war coming Edward revoked his homage for Aquitaine.

The issue of homage for Aquitaine should have been resolved by the Treaty of Brétigny of 1360 between Edward III and John II of France after the English victory at Poitiers in 1356. Under the treaty Edward III agreed to renounce his claim to the throne of France in return for French agreement that he should hold Aquitaine in full sovereignty. Unfortunately, King John II died before these terms were put into effect, and the issue remained in the forefront of the quarrel between England and France. In 1369 Charles V reclaimed sovereignty over Aquitaine and Edward III took up the title of King of France once more. In 1399, on his father's accession as Henry IV, the 13-year-old future Henry V was named Duke of Aquitaine, but the dispute over sovereignty came into sharp focus again in early 1401 when the French king, as a deliberate slight to Henry IV, named the Dauphin Louis, his eldest son and hence heir to the throne, Duke of Guienne (the French name for Aquitaine). The importance of resolving the dispute over sovereignty for Aquitaine was not lost on the young Henry, and it was a central tenet of his policy towards France after his accession in 1413.

The second cause of the war which was central to Henry's policy towards France was the claim of English kings to the crown of France. On the death of the French King Charles IV in 1328, the closest male successor was Edward III of England through his mother Isabella, sister to Charles IV and daughter of Philip IV.

The crux of the matter was whether the crown could be passed through the female line. The French view was that a woman could not inherit the crown and that she could not, therefore, pass this right to her son. Thus, Philip, the next closest male successor, who could trace his lineage back to Philip III through an unbroken male line, assumed the title of King Philip VI – the first of the Valois dynasty. There was a somewhat desultory attempt by the English to lay claim to the throne on behalf of the 15-year-old Edward III. This received short shrift in France, and there the matter lay until the third year of the war in 1340, when Edward formally laid claim to the crown of France.

It is not clear whether or not Edward held this claim as a serious war aim. Since, in the Treaty of Brétigny, he was prepared to trade the claim to the throne for sovereignty over Aquitaine it may have been simply a

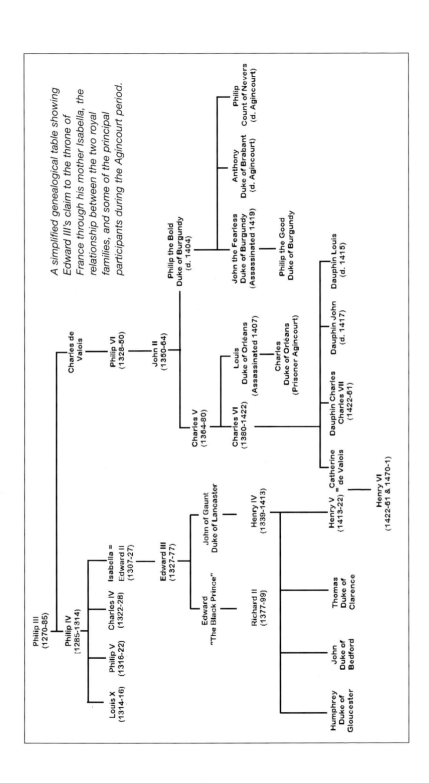

A simplified genealogical table showing Edward III's claim to the throne of France through his mother Isabella, the relationship between the two royal families, and some of the principal participants during the Agincourt period.

Philip III
(1270–85)

Philip IV
(1285–1314)

Charles de Valois

Louis X
(1314–16)

Philip V
(1316–22)

Charles IV
(1322–28)

Isabella =
Edward II
(1307–27)

Philip VI
(1328–50)

Edward III
(1327–77)

John II
(1350–64)

Edward
"The Black Prince"

John of Gaunt
Duke of Lancaster

Charles V
(1364–80)

Philip the Bold
Duke of Burgundy
(d. 1404)

Richard II
(1377–99)

Henry IV
(1339–1413)

Charles VI
(1380–1422)

Louis
Duke of Orléans
(Assassinated 1407)

John the Fearless
Duke of Burgundy
(Assassinated 1419)

Anthony
Duke of Brabant
(d. Agincourt)

Philip
Count of Nevers
(d. Agincourt)

Humphrey
Duke of Gloucester

John
Duke of Bedford

Thomas
Duke of Clarence

Henry V
(1413–22) =
Catherine
de Valois

Dauphin Charles
Charles VII
(1422–61)

Charles
Duke of Orléans
(Prisoner Agincourt)

Dauphin John
(d. 1417)

Philip the Good
Duke of Burgundy

Dauphin Louis
(d. 1415)

Henry VI
(1422–61 & 1470–1)

way of encouraging allies and exerting negotiating pressure on Philip VI and his successor John II. With the failure to implement the treaty the issue remained unresolved throughout the rest of Edward III's life and the reigns of Richard II and Henry IV, and the claim to the throne of France was a dominant war aim for Henry V.

The Outbreak of War and the English Ascendancy, 1337–1360

The conflict which broke out in 1337 under Edward III and Philip VI spanned the reigns of five French and five English kings before the war ended in 1453 with the expulsion of the English from all their French lands except the Calais enclave.

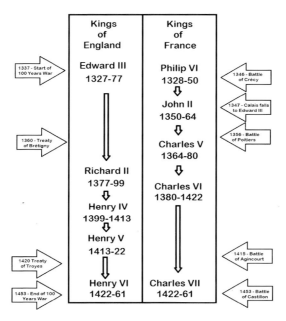

The first phase of the war, which was brought to a close by the Treaty of Brétigny in 1360, was marked by two significant English victories. In the first of these, at Crécy-en-Ponthieu in 1346, Edward III defeated Philip VI. The following year Edward took Calais after a protracted siege. The town, which remained in English hands until lost in 1558 during the reign of Mary I, gave the English kings an important foothold in France. A period of truce followed and the impact of the Black Death, which struck both France and England from 1348, also delayed a return to war.

The two countries remained at peace until the truce expired in 1355. The following year Edward III's eldest son, Edward the Black Prince, secured the second significant victory when he defeated a French army at Poitiers, capturing King John II and throwing France into chaos. Although Poitiers does not have the same high profile in English consciousness as Crécy and Agincourt, it was arguably the closest that the English came to winning a decisive battle during the Hundred Years War. Nevertheless, a further expedition to France led by Edward III was necessary in 1359–1360 to persuade the French to come to terms with the Treaty of Brétigny.

The Peace of Brétigny

Under the Treaty of Brétigny, in addition to Edward and John trading sovereignty over Aquitaine for the English claim to the French crown, huge tracts of south-western France were ceded to Edward. Thus the first phase of war left the English under Edward III in the ascendancy, but, due to the failure to implement all of its provisions, the Treaty of Brétigny, instead of providing the opportunity for a lasting peace, sowed the seeds for a renewal of war. On John's death in 1364 a substantial part of his ransom, agreed as part of the treaty, remained unpaid. This was still outstanding when Henry V came to the throne and payment was a further demand in his negotiations with the French.

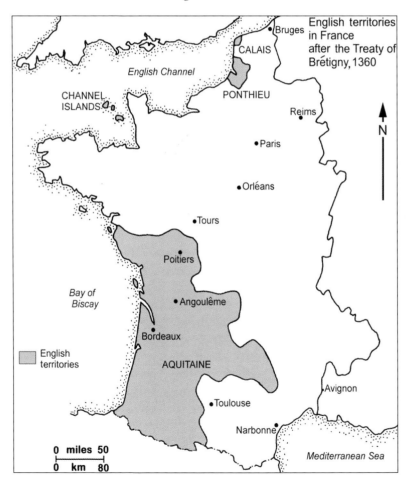

English territories in France after the Treaty of Brétigny, 1360

The French Recovery, 1369–1389

Charles V succeeded John II in 1364. He had been a party to the Treaty of Brétigny, but since the joint renunciations, of sovereignty over Aquitaine by John and by Edward of his claim to the French crown, had not been ratified he refused to be bound by them. From Charles' accession there was a steady deterioration in relations between France and England, and in 1367, at Nájera in Spain, an Anglo-Gascon army led by the Black Prince in support of Pedro the Cruel's claim to the throne of Castille defeated the other claimant, Henry of Trastámara and his Franco-Castilian army. Pedro reneged on his commitment to fund this campaign, and the Black Prince, who since 1363 had been Prince of Aquitaine, had to resort to increased taxation on his subjects in Aquitaine. This resulted in considerable discontent, and in 1368 the Count of Armagnac, whose lands lay within the newly expanded Aquitaine, appealed a dispute with the Black Prince to King Charles. Charles was aware that hearing the appeal amounted to a rejection of English claims to sovereignty over Aquitaine, but nevertheless he issued a summons for the prince to appear in Paris in 1369. The prince failed to attend and the war was renewed.

Charles V was too astute to repeat the experiences of his grandfather and father at the battles of Crécy and Poitiers, and he avoided set-piece battles. His strategy was to harass English armies and gradually push back the boundaries of English-held territory by retaking towns and castles. He was aided by a shrewd and effective commander, Bertrand du Guesclin, Constable of France, and by the time of Charles V's death in 1380 the English possessions had been reduced to the Calais Pale and a coastal strip near Bordeaux.

An Uneasy Truce, 1389–1415

The war continued, with neither side making significant advances, until the Truce of Leulinghem in 1389. Negotiations to find a permanent peace dragged on but without success, and in 1396, to forestall the risk of a return to war, an extension to the truce was agreed. The truce was cemented by the marriage of Richard II to Charles VI's daughter Isabella. However, trouble was in the wind, and in 1399 Henry Bolingbroke, son of John of Gaunt, usurped his cousin Richard II to become Henry IV. The French would not recognize Henry as the lawful King of England, but they did agree that the truce of 1396 would remain in force. Henry had his hands full at home with rebellions and trouble in Scotland and Wales, and the French, while stopping short of formally re-opening hostilities, missed no opportunity to create difficulties for the English, including incursions into Aquitaine, support for the Scots, recognition of Owen Glendower as Prince of Wales, and tacit support for acts of piracy against English shipping. From 1404 until early 1407 there were more determined, but unsuccessful, attempts to drive the English out of Aquitaine. Within the French camp, Charles VI suffered from sporadic bouts of mental illness which, although never making him totally incapable of ruling, left a major weakness at the heart of French government. This weakness was exacerbated by jockeying for power and feuding between the Duke of Orléans and his supporters, later known as the Armagnacs, and the Burgundians led by Duke John the Fearless. The Duke of Orléans, an erstwhile friend of Henry Bolingbroke while he had been in exile in France during the latter years of the reign of Richard II, turned violently against Henry after his usurpation of Richard, and he was the leading protagonist in attempts to drive the English from Aquitaine. The assassination of the Duke of Orléans in 1407 at the instigation of John the Fearless, successor to Philip the Bold as Duke of Burgundy, relieved the pressure on the English in Aquitaine but also resulted in a period of political instability and complex diplomatic relationships for the rest of the reign of Henry IV.

A triangular relationship emerged between the Armaganacs, the Burgundians and the English. Both French factions tried to gain English support as they manoeuvred for internal power, and the English attempted to exploit the weaknesses within France for their own ends. France descended into civil war during 1411 and 1412, with the English first of all intervening with an army led by the Earl of Arundel supporting the Duke of Burgundy and Charles VI against the rebel Armagnacs. In 1412 Henry IV, in response to a tempting offer from the Armagnacs that included recognition of English sovereignty over Aquitaine, sent an English army of 4,000 men led by the Duke of Clarence to support the rebels. However, by the time Clarence landed, the rebels, Charles VI and the Duke of Burgundy had come to terms and the competing factions were again at peace.

The Protagonists

Henry V was born in Monmouth in 1386, and might well have lived his life out as a nobleman, expecting to succeed to the titles of Earl of Derby and Hereford and Duke of Lancaster. However, in September 1399 his father Henry Bolingbroke usurped his cousin Richard II to become Henry IV. He immediately bestowed the traditional titles for the heir to the throne on his son: Prince of Wales, Duke of Cornwall and Earl of Chester. He also made him Duke of Aquitaine and Duke of Lancaster. Prince Henry could now look forward to becoming king in the course of time. He gained early experience of war and fought at the Battle of Shrewsbury in 1403, but much of his military experience in his youth was of small-scale, low-key operations in Wales. He had not been able to show his prowess against the French, a real enemy, and he felt that he had not been given the role that he deserved. As Prince Henry he may also have had a reputation for a somewhat dissolute lifestyle, immortalized in Shakespeare's plays. His youth was also coloured by an atmosphere of fear and insecurity as his father fought to hold on to the crown, and the young Henry feared for his own succession to the throne when a bad relationship developed with Henry IV in 1412, largely over differences in foreign policy. When Henry acceded to the throne in 1413 on the death of his father, in the words of Anne Curry, his experiences '. . . coloured his own approach to kingship and fanned his ambitions to prove himself and to prove his critics wrong. He was desperate for fame and success and would stop at nothing to achieve it.' He was deeply convinced of divine support for his cause, and he attributed his victory at Agincourt to the will of God and His punishment of the French. Henry's further successes in France in the years after Agincourt brought Henry close to achieving everything that he desired through the Treaty of Troyes in May 1420, which provided for him to become King of France on the death of Charles VI. Henry married Charles' daughter Catherine in June 1420. They had one child, the future Henry VI, and all seemed set fair. Then tragedy struck and Henry, described in Shakespeare's Henry VI Part I as 'too famous to live long', died two months before Charles in 1422. Historians are divided about his character. At one end of the scale he has been described as the greatest man that ever ruled England, while at the other end he has been labelled a deeply flawed individual, undermined by his own pride and overwhelmed by his own authority, lacking compassion, warmth and understanding of human frailty. However, whatever view is taken of his character, there can be few who would dispute that he was no ordinary man, and that he possessed extraordinary organizational skills, determination, leadership, personal courage and religious conviction.

Monmouth Castle, the birthplace of Henry V. (George Griffin)

Charles VI was born in Paris in 1368. During his childhood, his father Charles V made great progress in driving the English out of the lands that had been ceded to them under the Treaty of Brétigny. He had also begun to reform the French military system and brought order and stability to France. In his later years he made careful arrangements for the succession should he die while his young son was still a minor. But when the old king died in 1380 Christine de Pizan, a shrewd contemporary observer of events, commented that the accession of Charles VI at the age of 11 opened the gateway to French misfortunes. There was considerable reverence for, and obedience to, the king in French political life, and Charles VI was never under threat of usurpation, but the early years of his reign were marked by feuds and rivalry between his uncles: the Dukes of Berry, Anjou, Burgundy and Bourbon. Charles took power for himself in 1388, and there followed a brief period of order and prosperity. However, in 1392 the first signs of mental instability started to emerge. He was never totally incapable of ruling and he remained closely involved in government whenever his condition allowed. Nevertheless, throughout the remainder of his reign he was subject to periods of mental illness, and this, coupled with the rivalries between senior members of the royal family, led to France suffering from internal weakness and political instability throughout the remainder of his life. He married Isabeau of Bavaria in 1385, and they had twelve children. Their eldest daughter Isabella was Richard II's second wife for the last three years of his reign, and the youngest daughter, Catherine de Valois, married Henry V in 1420 after the Treaty of Troyes and was mother to Henry VI. Charles outlived Henry V by two months, thus denying him the French crown, and was known to posterity as the 'The Well-Beloved', for his success when he took power until the onset of his illness, and 'The Mad'. His fifth son became King Charles VII and brought the war to a successful conclusion for France, earning the nickname 'The Victorious'.

The thirteenth-century north door, known as the Valois door, of the basilica of St Denis in Paris – the final resting-place of French monarchs, including the Valois King Charles VI. (Peter Hoskins)

In March 1413 Henry IV died, and Prince Henry was crowned King Henry V. Because of his father's usurpation of Richard II and the subsequent history of rebellions against him during his reign as Henry IV, the new king could not feel entirely secure on his throne. However, the situation in France was even more precarious. In early 1414 the Duke of Burgundy had fallen from grace and was declared a traitor, and France once more descended into civil war with Charles VI, the dauphin and the Armagnacs launching a war against the Duke of Burgundy in Picardy and Artois between April and September. In January of the same year Henry had agreed a ten-year truce with the Duke of Brittany, declaring the duke to be an ally. Henry V had inherited from his father a campaign in Aquitaine being waged against the Armagnacs. This fighting came to a halt in early 1414, with a truce agreed to last for twelve months and applicable throughout France. Simultaneously Henry was putting out feelers for a lasting peace, with terms that included his marriage to Catherine de Valois, the daughter of Charles VI. This prospective marriage remained a central tenet of Henry's policy in the coming years. At Henry's coronation he had been anointed with oil that was said to carry the promise that kings blessed by it would recover lost English lands in France, including Normandy, and with France in disarray due to internecine fighting Henry felt emboldened enough by May 1414 to start to press his territorial claims on the French king. At about the same time, in parallel with his negotiations with Charles VI, he also appointed ambassadors to start negotiating an alliance with the Duke of Burgundy and a marriage to the duke's daughter. The focus of these negotiations was on an offensive alliance with mutual aid through the provision of men-at-arms and archers. The Duke of Burgundy was prepared to help Henry conquer lands held by the Armagnac lords, but he would not go so far as to enter into an alliance against Charles VI or the dauphin. By August it looked as though the Duke of Burgundy would not now oppose Henry's claim to the French crown and would, after all, be prepared to fight against King Charles, but he subsequently returned to negotiating a peace with Charles.

As Henry's ambassadors were negotiating with the Duke of Burgundy in August, others were pressing his case with Charles. The English opening gambit was to demand all of the rights claimed by Henry V, including the crown of France, but they agreed to discuss lesser terms without prejudice to Henry's claim to the throne. The main English demands were: the restitution of lands granted under the 1360 Treaty of Brétigny; homage and lordship over Normandy, Touraine, Maine and Anjou; and the homage of Brittany and Flanders. The 1.6 million écus outstanding from the Treaty of Brétigny for John II's ransom were also demanded, along with Henry's marriage to Charles' daughter Catherine with a dowry of 2 million écus. Henry's hope was that with the danger of an Anglo-Burgundian alliance hanging over them, Charles VI and his advisers could be pressured into accepting these terms. The French were certainly concerned over the English negotiations with the Duke of Burgundy, but they were not prepared to go as far as Henry wanted. His ambassadors returned empty-handed to England in October.

A Return to War, 1415–1444

Meanwhile, Henry had begun to prepare for war. Parliament had agreed to grant taxes to support his policy, but it wanted Henry to continue to negotiate. In pursuit of a negotiated peace, the truce, due to expire in January 1415, had been extended until May, and English ambassadors crossed to France once more in February. By the time of the arrival of the English negotiating team Charles VI and the Duke of Burgundy had come to terms and agreed the Treaty of Arras, which banned any alliances with the English that could be prejudicial to the interests of the French crown. When the negotiations reopened in March, Henry's ambassadors presented much reduced territorial demands and progress was made on the marriage between Henry and Catherine. The French, although their position had been much strengthened by the Duke of Burgundy's accommodation with the king, were ready to move some way towards Henry's demand over territories in Aquitaine. However, they linked this concession to withdrawal of the English claim for the sum outstanding from John II's ransom. The English ambassadors withdrew from negotiations towards the end of March, declaring that they did not have the authority to agree the terms on offer. Henry had so far failed to exploit the French divisions, but he continued to try to come to an accord with the Duke of Burgundy during the spring and summer, and the French continued to harbour fears of an Anglo-Burgundian alliance. They also sought to delay Henry's preparation for war, and French ambassadors crossed to England in June. Negotiations, which were held with Henry in person, broke down acrimoniously and the ambassadors returned to France in early July.

As the negotiations and preparations for war continued, Henry was acutely aware that his hold on the throne was insecure. Remarks made by the French ambassadors insinuated that not only did he have no right to the French crown, but also that they should be negotiating with descendants of Richard II and not Henry, and there was an apparent plot against him on the eve of his departure from the Solent on 1 August 1415 (the Southampton Plot), which resulted in the summary execution of the Earl of Cambridge, Henry Lord Scrope and Sir Thomas Grey.

Henry had intended to assemble his army by 1 July, but delays in mustering troops and gathering enough shipping delayed departure until 11 August. The landing was to be made in Normandy, probably with the objective of taking the duchy to strengthen Henry's bargaining position. Harfleur was the initial target, a useful bridgehead in northern France that would also deny the French use of an important fortified naval base, which had been used to launch attacks against the coast of England and on English shipping. Having taken Harfleur, Henry marched north-east towards Calais and safety. On reaching the Somme

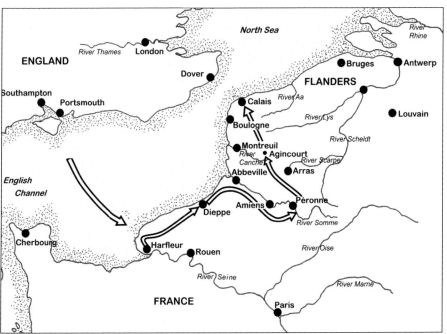

The Agincourt campaign.

he found the ford at Blanchetaque too well defended by the French and he marched up-river until he was able to cross. He turned once again towards Calais and confronted the French at Agincourt. After his victory he continued to Calais and returned to England. The story of the siege of Harfleur, the subsequent march through France and the Battle of Agincourt are described later in this guide. We now pick up the story after the king's return to England.

The Battle of Agincourt is popularly seen as the greatest English victory in the Middle Ages. However, despite the magnitude of the victory it was not decisive. Henry V's great-grandfather Edward III had been able to follow up his victory at Crécy with the siege and capture of Calais, and his great-uncle the Black Prince had captured John II at Poitiers, thus giving his father perhaps the closest that the English were to come to a decisive victory during the Hundred Years War. After Agincourt Charles VI remained at large, and Henry V did not have the means to follow up his victory that year. However, it did secure Henry's position on the throne so he could pursue his obsession with France unchallenged at home. He could now return to England and capitalize on his success and plan for the future.

During 1416 the Holy Roman Emperor Sigismund, who had initially offered to mediate between the French and the English, recognized Henry's claim to the French throne. Later in the year Sigismund and Henry met the Duke of Burgundy at Calais. Henry was encouraged that, while the Duke of Burgundy would not go so far as to recognize him as King of France, he would not stand in his way, and in August 1417 Henry set off again for France. His aim was to conquer the Duchy of Normandy and use it to enforce his claims. By the end of September Caen was in English hands. Other towns, including Bayeux, fell soon after and the conquest continued with Rouen, the greatest Norman city, falling in January 1419. The Duke of Burgundy was meanwhile taking advantage of the English operations to launch attacks against the Armagnacs. However, there was ambiguity in the Burgundian position and there were occasions when English and Burgundian troops clashed. The French were well aware that their disunity was playing into the hands of Henry V, and attempts were made to resolve the differences between the factions. In September the Duke of Burgundy met the dauphin. Heated discussions ensued and Duke John the Fearless was murdered by a member of the dauphin's party, thus precipitating the very event that the dauphin wished to avoid: pushing Burgundy, now ruled by the new duke, Philip the Good, into the arms of the English. In December 1419 Henry and Philip agreed to wage war together against the dauphin. They also agreed that if Henry succeeded in his pursuit of his claim to the French crown the Duke of Burgundy would be his lieutenant for his French domains.

Henry now turned his attention to King Charles VI with negotiations that concluded with the Treaty of Troyes in May 1420. Under the treaty the dauphin was declared a bastard and his claim to the succession set aside. Henry was to be heir to Charles VI and to be regent of France during the remainder of Charles's life. He was to retain the Duchy of Normandy by right of conquest in the meantime, and his entitlement to hold Aquitaine without homage was recognized. Little more than a week after the treaty Henry married Charles' daughter Catherine. Henry and Philip then took Sens and Montereau, and besieged Melun, which fell in November 1420. Henry now returned to England leaving the Duke of Clarence as his lieutenant.

The dauphin, who was by no means powerless, had been consolidating his position. In response to the dauphin invoking the 'auld alliance' with Scotland, a number of Scots had entered his service, and at Easter 1421 the Duke of Clarence was killed when he was defeated at Baugé by a Franco-Scottish army. In June Henry V returned to France, and, while the Duke of Burgundy fought the dauphin's forces in Picardy, he marched first to Paris and then to Meaux, which he besieged. In December Henry's heir, the future Henry VI, was born, but before a year had passed Henry V died of dysentery in August 1422. Less than two months later Charles VI followed him to the grave. The infant Henry VI was proclaimed King of England and France.

Henry V's untimely death at the age of 35 left his brother the Duke of Bedford as regent in France. Under his regency there were further English victories, but the duke was faced with a range of problems as he struggled to build on Henry's legacy and consolidate English rule in France. He and the Duke of Burgundy controlled large areas of France, but outside these areas France was loyal to the dauphin, and Bedford struggled to make further inroads into this territory. He also faced growing discontent from Henry VI's subjects in France who were compelled to pay taxes to support the war, and a similar reluctance at home to pay for the continuing fighting. Difficulties with his allies compounded his problems. The Duke of Brittany moved back and forth between the French and English causes and the Duke of Burgundy was reluctant to pursue the war vigorously.

Then in 1429 Joan of Arc came onto the scene. Joan brought a change of fortune for the French. The siege of Orléans was broken in May, and the retreating English army was defeated at the Battle of Patay the following month. The dauphin, at Joan's urging, went to Rheims and was crowned and anointed as Charles VII, giving a further boost to his standing and French morale. The capture of Joan in 1430 and her

subsequent trial and execution in 1431 offered the prospect of restored English fortunes, and the Duke of Bedford brought Henry VI to Paris to be crowned King of France in December. However, lack of funds from England to prosecute the war and the continuing necessity of imposing taxes on the inhabitants of Normandy led to increasing discontent among the population and an erosion of English control. The following year the Duke of Burgundy was beginning to look for ways to break with the English. In 1435 the Duke of Bedford died, and only two weeks after his death Philip the Good finally made peace with Charles VII.

The Truce of Tours, 1444–1449, and the Defeat of the English

The war continued, with the French making inroads into English-held lands, and by 1444 the areas held by the English had been reduced to part of Aquitaine, the Calais enclave, Lower Normandy and the County of Maine. But by now both sides were ready for peace, and the Truce of Tours was agreed. The truce collapsed in 1449. The English were rapidly swept aside and by April 1450 all of Henry V's gains in northern France had gone. The French now turned their attention to Bordeaux and Aquitaine, and in July 1453 an Anglo-Gascon army was routed at Castillon, in the last battle of the Hundred Years War. Three months later Bordeaux surrendered and the war was over.

At first sight it may seem strange that the English kings should win the three great battles of Crécy, Poitiers and Agincourt, as well as many less well known battles, and yet lose the war. We can never know what would have happened if Henry V had outlived Charles VI. However, with the benefit of hindsight it is difficult to see how English kings could have held on to power in France. France was significantly richer and more populous than England. Edward III overcame these imbalances in population and wealth through victories on the battlefields at Crécy and Poitiers, the exploitation of internal divisions in France, and his effective use of contracted armies. The inherent weakness of the English position became apparent after the collapse of the Treaty of Brétigny in 1369, when Edward had to hold vastly expanded territories while Charles V avoided pitched battles and recovered towns and castles slowly but surely. By Henry V's time the French internal divisions were even more acute than during Edward III's reign, and in alliance with the Duke of Burgundy he was able to take advantage of French weakness to conquer and hold wide swathes of territory. However, in Henry VI's reign holding these lands imposed an intolerable burden of taxation both at home and in the English territories in France. In addition, French military reforms came to fruition under Charles VII, resulting in a more professional army that made good use of its artillery to reduce the last English strongholds and bring Charles' army victory at Castillon. The internal divisions within France were also gradually mastered. Once this process had been completed and French resources could be effectively used, the expulsion of the English from France was probably inevitable. Within two years of the Battle of Castillon England became embroiled in the Wars of the Roses, and with the energies of English kings and the nobility turned inwards there was no way back. Perhaps Agincourt has gained a disproportionate importance in English culture, but this cannot detract from a great victory against the odds which owed much to the personal determination and leadership of Henry V.

Tour One

Le Havre and the Siege of Harfleur

This tour starts in the modern town of Le Havre, covering the short distance from the landing of Henry V and his army near Ste-Adresse, now part of the agglomeration of Le Havre, on 14 August 1415 to the town of Harfleur, which was besieged until its surrender on 22 September 1415. It covers a distance of 14km.

What Happened
The Landing and the Siege of Harfleur
During the summer of 1415 Henry V gathered his army in the area around Southampton. The army was around 12,000 strong. In round figures 2,500 were men-at-arms and the remainder archers. There were also gunners, with thirty or so recruited from outside England. In addition to the combatants there are known to have been 560 men employed as miners, carpenters, stonemasons, labourers, smiths and waggoners. There would certainly, however, have been many more non-combatants, with the personal households of the king and his great

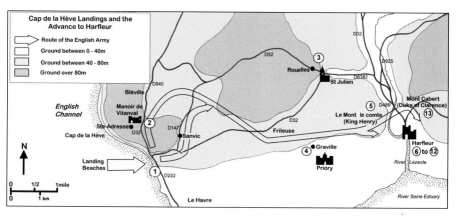

lords, pages for the men-at-arms, and tradesmen and artisans of all sorts including fletchers, armourers and bowyers. The numbers cannot be quantified with any certainty but an estimate of an overall total of 15,000 combatants and non-combatants is probably on the conservative side. There would also have been wagons to carry supplies, the personal baggage of the king and the senior members of the army, and spare arrows, bows and bowstrings. In addition, there was the artillery train to be used at the siege of Harfleur. And of course there were horses. The number of horses would certainly have exceeded the number of men, with knights taking typically four horses on campaign, esquires three, men-at-arms two and mounted archers one. To carry this army a fleet of around 1,500 ships of varying sizes and types had assembled in the Solent off Southampton. Despite its size even this fleet was not sufficient. Some of the army had to be left behind at the outset, although they may have followed on later since there were replacements present in the army after the siege of Harfleur.

The modern ferry crossing from Portsmouth to Le Havre takes four hours, but for Henry it would take the best part of two days. Henry's fleet sailed on 11 August 1415 and entered the mouth of the river Seine two days later, dropping anchor at around 5.00 p.m. on 13 August off a small hamlet called 'Kidecaus'. This was the small port of St-Denis-Chef-de-Caux on the headland to the north-west of the Seine estuary near Cap de la Hève. In 1374 the village, which in the fourteenth century had been a relatively important fortified port, had been carried away into the sea by storms and high tides. St-Denis-Chef-de-Caux was rebuilt further inland and later given its current name of Ste-Adresse. The port seems to have remained useful into the fifteenth century, although it gradually fell into disuse and it may have been little more than a sheltered landing place when Henry arrived off the coast. According to a contemporary account, the landing area was very stony with large boulders that were dangerous for ships. Behind the shore lay deep, water-filled ditches, and beyond these thick earth walls with ramparts. There was also a marshy area towards Harfleur, and on the high ground stood the castle of Vitanval (Point 2). Thus, the area was readily defensible, and yet there were no French troops to hinder the landing.

The king gave strict instructions for the disembarkation and ordered that no one was to land before he did so. This instruction was probably given to ensure that the landing was controlled and that troops did not disperse in search of plunder. Nevertheless, the king prudently sent a small reconnaissance party ashore early on the morning of 14 August to ensure that the area immediately inland from the landing beaches was clear of enemy forces. The main disembarkation began in the afternoon, and was not completed until three days later on 17 August. The king immediately made his way towards high ground, and spent his first night ashore on the high ground between the coast and Harfleur, possibly lodging in the priory of Graville, with the Dukes of Clarence and Gloucester nearby.

Today the north bank of the Seine estuary from Le Havre to Harfleur and beyond has been developed into a major port complex. In 1415 the estuary of the Seine and its hinterland were very different from what we see today. The port of Le Havre was not created until 1517, due to Harfleur having become increasingly silted up, and the modern port has absorbed the coastline on the north bank of the river. In the fifteenth century there was another port further along the estuary to the east of Le Havre, lying south-west of Harfleur at l'Eure. This survives solely as a place name, the port having been destroyed during the Hundred Years War and subsequently absorbed into Le Havre.

The coast north of the lighthouse at Cap de la Hève (GPS 49.511717, 0.067731) fits the contemporary description well, but there is no easy exit from the shore along this stretch of coastline over the steep cliffs rising 100m above sea level. Furthermore, there would have been little point in constructing ditches and walls here, given the natural defences provided by the cliffs. However, 1.5km to the south-east of Cap de la Hève, between Ste-Adresse and the modern yachting marina, or Port de Plaisance (GPS 49.489901, 0.097525), there is a relatively wide extent of flat land (Point 1), and the coast becomes less rocky. A landing here would be much more feasible than further north over dangerous rocks below the cliffs. This also fits well with the contemporary account of the landing being made within the mouth of the Seine. The flat land extends to the east across the modern town and port of Le Havre, and it is probable that this is where the defences had been prepared with the marsh a short distance beyond. The difficulty of crossing the marsh, which was emphasized in the contemporary account, would explain why the army then climbed up on to the high ground for the advance to Harfleur. This landing place also allowed easy access from the shore

This view looks north from the likely landing beach towards Ste-Adresse. Cap de la Hève is on the extreme left, and the routes onto the high ground climb from just left of the centre of the photograph. (Peter Hoskins)

along two routes inland onto the high ground. Nevertheless, moving the heavy equipment and cannon off the beaches and onto the ridge would have been a laborious and time-consuming process.

As with the shore line of the estuary, the hinterland has been developed a great deal over the centuries. The high ground to the north of the river extends to the east for about 10km from the Cap de la Hève and then falls rapidly into the valley of the river Lézarde and the town of Harfleur. In 1415 the area was largely open with cultivated land, hamlets and orchards, and scrub woodland on the slopes towards the river below the modern Rue Georges Lafaurie, Rue du 329ème Régiment d'Infanterie and Rue Salvador Allende. There were a number of settlements, including Sanvic, Ingouville, Bléville, Graville and Rouelles (Point 3), which have now all been absorbed into the residential areas of Le Havre. At Graville, 2.5km west of Harfleur and just below the crest of the escarpment, stood the church of Ste Honorine and its priory, where Henry V is said to have lodged (Point 4), and there was a castle on the cliffs overlooking the Seine. A similar distance north-east of Graville is Mont Lecomte (Point 5), where Henry V sited his siege camp with a commanding view down into the town of Harfleur 1.5km to the south-east. On the night of 18 August the Duke of Clarence was sent to the east of Harfleur with the vanguard. He set up his camp to the north of the town on Mont Cabert (Point 13), also with a commanding view of the town.

Harfleur lies in the valley of the river Lézarde, between high ground close by to the west and east. There is further high ground just over 1km to the north towards Montivilliers. To the south, towards the Seine, the ground has long since been drained and developed, but in 1415 this was marshland. The river Lézarde runs south through the town from Montivilliers. By damming the river where it entered Harfleur, the townspeople were able to cause it to burst its banks and flood the area between the western walls and the high ground. The sluice gates had been closed when news of the English landings reached the town, and by the time Henry reached Harfleur the water was already thigh deep. As a consequence, Clarence's deployment to the east of the town required his men to skirt round well to the north, covering a distance of

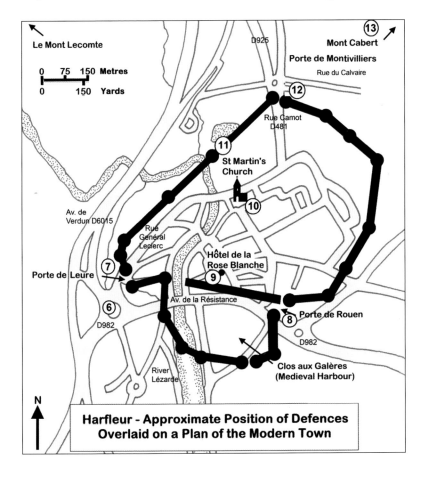

Harfleur – Approximate Position of Defences Overlaid on a Plan of the Modern Town

about 16km. The town was defended by walls 2,900m long with twenty-two interval towers, water-filled ditches perhaps 4.5m deep with steep banks, and three gates. To the west was the Porte de Leure (Point 7), to the north the Porte de Montivilliers (Point 12) and to the south-east the Porte de Rouen (Point 8). All the gates were well protected by outworks. Those protecting the western gate, Porte de Leure, were recorded by a witness to the siege. They were constructed of tree trunks lashed together and driven into the ground, with earth and further wood inside to add strength. They were pierced with embrasures for small guns and cross-bows.

The walls were relatively modern, having been built between 1344 and 1361, and they appear to have been kept in repair. The defences were further enhanced by the fortified port, Le Clos des Galées or Clos aux Galères, to the south of the town. The entrance to the port was defended with chains drawn across the entrance channel between two towers. A Spanish sailor reported in 1405 that the defences included a good wall with strong towers, town gates all protected by draw-bridges flanked by towers, and water-filled ditches with steep sides built of stone. The town was equipped with artillery, and no doubt had stocks of catapults and large crossbows. The townsfolk had also prepared for a possible attack by stockpiling wood and stones, and it seems that they may have torn up the paving slabs from the causeway leading north towards Montivilliers to supplement their materials for maintaining the defences.

Harfleur is likely to have had a militia drawn from the population, and there were also some crossbowmen and men-at-arms. Reinforcements arrived on 18 August, probably entering through the Porte de Rouen, before Clarence could complete the investment of the town. The defence was in the hands of Louis, the Sire d'Estouteville, and Raoul de Gaucourt. Based on accounts relating to the surrender, some 260 knights and men-at-arms were allowed to leave when the town capitulated, and it is probable that this was roughly the number of men-at-arms in the town during the siege.

Harfleur was well known to the English. It was an important commercial and naval port and had been used for piratical raids and operations against English shipping and south coast towns. It had been attacked unsuccessfully by the English in April 1360, but in the following month Edward III had embarked from here after the negotiations leading to the Treaty of Brétigny. Furthermore, Ste-Adresse had been raided in 1369 by John of Gaunt and Harfleur had been attacked unsuccessfully in 1378 by Richard Fitzalan, Earl of Arundel, and John Montague, Earl of Salisbury. More recently Henry V's ambassadors had passed through the port on their return to England in 1414. No doubt they would have taken the opportunity to assess the defences.

Henry had started his investment of Harfleur on 17 August, and by 23 August the siege was sufficiently well established for the inhabitants to send word to Charles d'Albret, the Constable of France, in Rouen that they could no longer make contact by land. They asked for a boat to be provided to help with the provisioning of the town and to enable messages to be passed between the besieged town and the constable. D'Albret arranged for a small galley, which had the advantage of being powered by oars, to be sent downstream on the Seine from Rouen.

At some stage early in the siege Henry offered terms to Harfleur. A chaplain with the army, the author of Gesta Henrici Quinti, a detailed account of the campaign, remarked that these terms were in accordance with the Book of Deuteronomy: either peace in return for surrender or, if the town had to be taken by assault, no quarter for the male inhabitants, with women and property liable to be carried off as spoils of war. The offer was rejected and a bombardment of the town began, which over the duration of the siege caused considerable damage both to the town defences and to the houses – so much so that the repairs to the fortifications took a number of years and the poor state of the buildings within the town proved to be a strong disincentive when Henry was seeking to encourage English people to settle there. It is indicative of the destruction that, although there are a number of domestic buildings in the town surviving from the fifteenth century, their construction is generally attributed to the latter part of the century.

Maintaining a large army besieging a town was always likely to be problematic, because of the risk of disease and the difficulties of feeding men and horses. Raids into the surrounding countryside were necessary. French troops in the vicinity kept the foraging parties under close surveillance, harrying them when they had the opportunity, and they may well also have adopted a scorched earth policy in the surrounding area to hamper English provisioning.

As the siege progressed Henry moved on to enforce a blockade with ships on the Seine and smaller boats in the area flooded by the Lézarde.

By mid-September the cordon around the town by land and water was beginning to bite, and an attempt was made to break the stranglehold between 14 and 16 September with a small fleet sent from Rouen. The attempt was unsuccessful, and by 18 September the town decided to enter into negotiations for surrender. Meanwhile, although it would not prejudice the success of the siege, Henry was having problems due to insanitary conditions brought on by unseasonably warm weather, polluted water, difficulties in disposing of carcasses and other rubbish and the generally humid conditions. The result was dysentery, which had a serious impact on some parts of the army, leading to the deaths, amongst others, of the Bishop of Norwich and the Earl of Suffolk.

At some point during the siege the English had managed to cut off the flow of water from the Lézarde somewhere between Harfleur and Montivilliers. As a result the flood water had subsided, and the besieging forces were able to move closer to the town on the southern and western sides. The English also constructed trenches to defend the besiegers from fire from the town, and hoardings were made which sheltered guns and gunners and were lifted when the guns were to be fired. Clarence's men were approximately where the Rue du Calvaire runs today and isolated from the bulk of the army and, because of the high ground behind them, close up to the walls. Thus, they were particularly vulnerable, and their trenches were especially important. Although the French made no serious attempt to relieve the town, there were engagements between the besieging army and French troops from the garrison, and possibly from nearby Montivilliers. As early as 18 August Clarence and his men had come under attack while they deployed to the east of the town. There was a further sortie by the garrison on 15 September. An attack was made on the English defences constructed to the west of the town near the Leure gate, roughly where the car park now stands at the junction of the Rue de l'Eure and Rue des Remparts. It is possible that this was a diversionary attack timed to coincide with the attempt to break the waterborne blockade. It caused some embarrassment since the French were able to set fire to the English trench works, but the impact was limited. Henry decided on a riposte, and overnight preparations were made for an attack the next day. In the morning the Earl of Huntingdon drove the French back from the barbican and inside the main walls.

During the siege Henry's attempts to wear down the defences with guns and catapults had some success. However, at night the French carried out repairs using timber and tubs filled with earth, dung, sand and stones, and walls were shored up with faggots, earth and clay. Streets were also covered with sand to prevent stone cannon balls splintering on impact. These efforts could do no more than delay the destruction of the defences, however, and eventually the outer barbicans were abandoned with their guns being repositioned inside. There was also an attempt by Clarence's men to undermine the walls on the eastern side of the town. This may have been a reflection of the lack of effect of the artillery fire, or it may have been due to better conditions for mining on this side of the town. In any case, in the face of French counter-mining and sorties to disrupt the work, the attempt was unsuccessful and the mine was abandoned and subsequently filled in during the English occupation.

Henry made several attempts to negotiate the surrender of Harfleur, but initially the French garrison believed that an army was being mustered to relieve the town. By 17 September it had become clear that the chances of relief were remote. It is not clear whether the garrison then sought to surrender or whether Henry took the initiative and offered terms. Whatever the case, the negotiations collapsed, and Henry made preparations for an assault the following day. This was preceded by a call to arms by trumpet and by an all-night bombardment. The defenders decided that enough was enough, and it seems that a message was passed through Clarence asking for terms. The king sent in the Earl of Dorset, Lord Fitzhugh and Sir Thomas Erpingham to negotiate terms. Henry had wanted the surrender to be made the following day, but he conceded that more time could be given to the inhabitants. The result was that the town would be surrendered if either Charles VI or the dauphin did not come to its relief by 1.00 p.m. on Sunday, 22 September.

Although Henry had left the negotiations to others, he took the surrender in person in his pavilion on Mont Lecomte. In a manner in keeping with the customs of the time, Henry behaved graciously and entertained members of the garrison, including de Gaucourt. The Earl of Dorset was appointed captain of the town, and the next day Henry entered Harfleur, dismounting on entering the town, to give thanks to God in the church of St Martin (Point 10). The French captains were free to go, subject to agreeing under oath to submit themselves at Calais on 11 November. De Gaucourt was despatched to carry a challenge from the king to the dauphin. Civilians were separated into two groups: those swearing fealty to Henry, and those being retained in custody against payment of ransoms. Women, children, the poor and the helpless, numbering between 1,500 and 2,000, were expelled from the town on 24 September, in part because the town was in no condition to support the population. They took with them their clothing, all that they could carry, and five sous (shillings in English pre-decimal currency). They were escorted by the English to Lillebonne, 32km to the east, where they were handed over to Marshal Boucicaut, who gave them food and water.

Henry wished to establish Harfleur as an English colony on a similar basis to Calais. His first step was to arrange for a garrison of 300 men-at-arms and 900 archers. He also took steps to encourage settlement. Municipal records and title deeds were burned in the market place and henceforth purchase and inheritance of land were restricted to Englishmen, French inhabitants being reduced to the status of lessees. On 5 October the Duke of Bedford, who had remained in England as keeper of the realm, reinforced these provisions, ordering the sheriffs of London to proclaim that all merchants, victuallers and artificers who were willing to reside in Harfleur should go with all speed to the town, where they would be given houses. Orders were also sent out for the repair of the town and for its provisioning from England. The town remained in English hands until it was recaptured by the French in 1435. The English recovered Harfleur in 1440, but finally surrendered it to the French on Christmas Eve, 1449.

The French Response

The French had taken some preliminary measures to counter the anticipated English landing, but could not realistically have mobilized a large army before Henry arrived. However, even by the due date for Harfleur's surrender on 22 September the forces available were insufficient to relieve the town.

In June the French nobility, and those others accustomed to bearing arms, had been given notice to prepare themselves to rally to the defence of France. Shortly after the start of the siege of Harfleur the Constable of France, Charles d'Albret, had sent word to the king and the dauphin in Paris of the arrival of Henry. On 28 August the nobility in Normandy and the surrounding areas were called to arms. Rouen was nominated as the point of rendezvous, and the dauphin was sent to Normandy as the king's lieutenant and Captain General as the French army began to gather. The king indicated his intention to follow soon to raise the siege. Orders were also given to ensure that castles were adequately defended. The first proclamation to communicate these decisions was issued on 30 August in Paris, and over the next ten days it was posted in other places in the Ile-de-France, Picardy and Normandy. Arrangements to raise taxes for the war had been put in place in March, but on 31 August the king's council ordered additional taxes to be raised to cover the costs of the gathering army. The taxes envisaged an army of 6,000 men-at-arms and 3,000 archers. On 10 September the king attended mass in the cathedral of St-Denis and the *oriflamme*, the banner used in battle to signify that no quarter would be given, was entrusted to Guillaume VIII Martel, the Sire de Bacqueville. In the event, since the king was not present at Agincourt, Guillaume did not carry the *oriflamme* at the battle. His lands lay on the route Henry would eventually take when he left Harfleur and Guillaume was to meet his death at Agincourt fighting on the left wing under the command of the Count of Vendôme at more than 60 years of age.

In early September news reached the dauphin that Harfleur was in desperate need of reinforcement. By 13 September he had reached Vernon on the river Seine, and here he received envoys carrying news of the plight of Harfleur. The envoys were assured that the king was gathering his army and would come to their aid. This was partially true, to the extent that the king was indeed assembling his army, but by the date of the agreement of terms for the surrender of Harfleur there were no more than a few thousand men available. Furthermore, they were dispersed across several locations to enable the French to respond to possible English movements, and were not in a position to relieve Harfleur before the due date for its surrender. Once the terms of the surrender had been agreed on 18 September, the Sire de Hacqueville set out to notify the dauphin and ask for assistance. When he arrived at Vernon, the dauphin broke the news that the assembly of the army was not complete and assistance would not be forthcoming. However, given that Hacqueville probably took two days to reach the dauphin at Vernon, even if the French army had assembled, relief of the town before 22 September would not have been possible.

The Route by Car

The likely landing beaches run alongside the D232, Boulevard Albert I, in Le Havre to the north-west of the ferry port (Point 1). Looking towards Ste-Adresse, the two exits from the beach can be seen. One of these follows the D32 and D147 below the walls of the fort, and the other the D940 to the west up onto the high ground near Bléville, close to the Manoir de Vitanval (Point 2). The D982 is the most direct route to Harfleur, with a short deviation along the Avenue Pablo Picasso to visit the priory of Graville (Point 4).

To visit the Manoir de Vitanval, Graville, the church of St Julien in Rouelles (Point 3) and Mont Lecomte (Point 5), leave Ste-Adresse on the D79. The Manoir is just off this road a little over 1km north of Ste-Adresse. Return to Ste-Adresse and take the D982 towards Harfleur. Turn left onto the Avenue Pablo Picasso to visit the priory at Graville. After visiting the priory, return to the Avenue Pablo Picasso, take the Rue d'Aplemont and then turn left onto Avenue Paul Bert. Follow this road and then the Rue de Rouelles and Rue Socrate to the junction with the D32. Turn right to Rouelles to visit St Julien. Retrace your route along the D32 and Rue Socrate to the junction with the Avenue du 8 mai 1945. Follow this road and then the Rue Edouard Vaillant to park close to the Maison de l'Enfance Ferme du Mont Lecomte to visit Mont Lecomte. To continue to Harfleur follow the Rue Edouard Vaillant and turn right onto Avenue du Monte Lecomte. Turn left and follow Avenue de Général Ferrié d'Aplemont and the D982 to Harfleur.

The Route on Foot and by Bike

The walking and cycling route is through urban areas, predominantly along minor roads but with a short distance on a path. The overall distance is 14km.

From Ste-Adresse (Point 1) the walker needs to climb up onto the ridge above Le Havre to join the Rue Georges Lafaurie, which in turn becomes the Rue du 329ème Régiment d'Infanterie, Rue Salvador Allende and then Rue Pablo Neruda. There is a variety of options for this using the roads and numerous staircases that cut off some tortuous hairpin bends. The priory of Graville (Point 4) can be visited by making a short descent from the Rue Pablo Neruda just before the road becomes Rue Andrei Sakharov. There are signs to the priory, but these are intended for vehicles and a better route for the walker is down the

Escalier de l'Abbaye, just after the intersection of the Rue Eugène Boudin with Rue Pablo Neruda.

> *Cyclists wishing to visit the priory of Graville will need to either carry their bicycles down the Escalier de l'Abbaye or follow the signposted route for vehicles.*

Leave the priory gardens through the gate at the eastern end and then follow the Rue de l'Abbaye, Rue Corot, Passage Stanley and Avenue Pablo Picasso to cross the Rue Andrei Sakharov. Follow the Rue d'Aplemont and Rue Lieutenant Clerivet to the crossing of the Avenue du Général Ferrié d'Aplemont, where the way-marks of the *GR2 Variante* can be followed towards Harfleur. The path meets the Chemin de Cauchaville. After about 150m, turn right onto the Rue de la Gaieté to pass under the railway and the D6015 to join the D231, which then runs into the roundabout with the statue of Jehan de Grouchy in the centre (Point 6). Access to the town of Harfleur is along either the Rue de l'Eure or the Rue des Remparts off the D481 or along the Avenue de la Résistance (D982).

> *The section of the GR2 Variante on the route between Graville and Harfleur is a steep grass path. An alternative route for cyclists is to take the Rue Andrei Sakharov and then the Avenue du Général Ferrié d'Aplemont to join the D982 to Harfleur.*

What to See
Le Havre
Point 1: The likely landing beaches run alongside the D232, Boulevard Albert I, in Le Havre to the north-west of the ferry port in the suburb of Ste-Adresse (GPS 49.501357, 0.087669).

Point 2: The Manoir de Vitanval (GPS 49.511259, 0.083685) stands at the junction of the Rue de la Solitude and the Rue du Manoir in Ste-Adresse. The Manoir was built later in the fifteenth century to replace a castle that was on the site in 1415. The castle was garrisoned by the English from 1419.

The fifteenth-century Manor of Vitanval. (Peter Hoskins)

The church of St Julien in Rouelles. (Peter Hoskins)

Point 3: The church of St Julien (GPS 49.522346, 0.162767), Rue Maurice Blard in Rouelles, one of the settlements along the line of advance of the English army after their landing, was first recorded in 1035 under the patronage of the abbey of Montivilliers. It has been much modified over the centuries but the nave survives from the thirteenth century.

Point 4: The eleventh-century church of Ste Honorine and the thirteenth-century monastic buildings of the priory of Graville (GPS 49.503559, 0.164881) survive in Rue de l'Abbaye. The priory is said to have been used by Henry V for his lodgings during the siege of Harfleur. It now houses a museum: http://lehavre.fr/node/95. Access by car is via the Rue de l'Abbaye off the Avenue Pablo Picasso. Within the lordship of Graville was the manor of Frileuse, now a residential area about 1.5km north-west of the priory, which in 1416 was granted by Henry V to John Fastolf, who had been in the retinue of the Earl of Suffolk in 1415 and was subsequently with the English garrison of Harfleur.

The priory of Graville. (Peter Hoskins)

Point 5: The siege camp of Henry V was sited on Mont Lecomte. The area remains largely undeveloped and access can be gained by parking near the Stade Jules Ladoumèque in the Rue Edouard Vaillant (GPS 49.513611, 0.18). The Rue Edouard Vaillant stretches over some distance, but there is parking close to the Maison de l'Enfance Ferme du Mont Lecomte and the Parc de la Ferme du Mont Lecomte, both of which are well signposted. From the car park follow the path signposted towards the Parc, and turn sharp right just beyond the Maison de l'Enfance. Unfortunately the view that Henry V would have had down into the valley of the Lézarde and over Harfleur is obscured by trees, but an impression can still be gained of the dominant position of the site 80m above the besieged town.

Harfleur

Point 6: In the centre of the roundabout at the western end of the Avenue de la Résistance (GPS 49.504579, 0.195447) is a statue of Jehan de Grouchy. De Grouchy was at the head of the French troops that retook the town in 1435. He lost his life in the fighting at the age of 81.

Point 7: The Porte de Leure to the west has long since disappeared, but was near the intersection of the Rue des Remparts and the Rue de l'Eure (GPS 49.505294, 0.195769).

Point 8: Of the three town gates only the Porte de Rouen (GPS 49.504695, 0.201815), on the Rue du Pont de Rouen, survives. The remains are largely of later fifteenth-century construction, but the layout can be clearly

Jehan de Grouchy. (Peter Hoskins)

seen. The gate was a complex structure serving three purposes: one gate giving external access, a second gate serving as a postern for access to the port and a third allowing access between the port and the town. The old medieval port to which the gate gave access, le Clos aux Galères, which was also protected by walls, was to the south of the town but has long since been filled in and built over.

The remains of the Porte de Rouen. (Peter Hoskins)

The Hôtel de la Rose Blanche. (Peter Hoskins)

Point 9: The Hôtel de la Rose Blanche (GPS 49.505889, 0.189315), in the Rue Jehan de Grouchy, now houses the library. It has elements dating from the fourteenth century, but was developed during the fifteenth, seventeenth and eighteenth centuries. It is said that the captain of the town's garrison lived here in the fifteenth century, but it is not clear whether or not this was before the siege in 1415 or during later periods, including perhaps the English occupations between 1415 and 1435, and 1440 and 1449.

Point 10: After the town surrendered Henry V gave thanks in the parish church of St Martin (GPS 49.507084, 0.199610) in the Rue des Cent-Quatre (named after the 104 citizens of Harfleur who opened the gates to attacking French troops in 1435). There are some minor elements dating from the eleventh century, but much of the church was destroyed

The church of St Martin. (Peter Hoskins)

during a subsequent English assault on the town in 1440. Most of the current building dates from the late fifteenth and early sixteenth centuries.

Point 11: Vestiges of the town walls survive on the north-west side of the town. They can be visited on foot, just beyond the end of the Rue du Moulin (GPS 49.50823, 0.198934).

Remains of the Harfleur town walls near the Rue du Moulin. (Peter Hoskins)

Point 12: The Porte de Montivilliers no longer exists but was near a roundabout in the modern Rue Carnot in the north of the town. There is a small parking area just south of the roundabout on the east side of the Rue Carnot (GPS 49.509348, 0.201567). Close to the car park a

A section of surviving wall close to the site of the Porte de Montivilliers gate. (Peter Hoskins)

Traces of the town ditch, between the walls and the position of the Duke of Clarence's men, with vestiges of a small tower. (Peter Hoskins)

section of the ditch that formed part of the defences of the town can be clearly seen, with a small section of wall nearby. About 100m further along the ditch are the remains of a tower.

Point 13: The siege camp of the Duke of Clarence was sited at Mont Cabert (GPS 49.514399, 0.207067). As with the king's camp on the other side of the valley of the Lézarde, Mont Cabert is in a dominant position 80m above the town. The view of Harfleur is obscured by trees, but Mont Lecomte can be clearly seen from the Duke of Clarence's camp, which gives a clear indication of the commanding positions of the two camps. To get to the site take the D6015 from Harfleur. Leave the D6015 and follow signs for Parc de l'Estuaire Ouest. At the first roundabout, turn right onto the Avenue du Cantipou. Turn left at the second roundabout into the Rue de la Crête. Access can be gained to Mont Cabert on foot from the end of the road.

Maps

Maps at 1:25,000, 1:50,000 and 1:100,000 Scales	
Published by the *Institut National de l'Information Géographique et Forestière (IGN)* www.ign.fr	
Cartes de Randonnée – 1:25,000	
1710ET – Le Havre	
Série Orange – 1:50,000	
M1710 - Montivilliers	M1711 – Le Havre
TOP 100 – 1:100,000	
TOP100107 – Rouen/Le Havre	

How to Get There and Back by Public Transport

Deauville, Beauvais and Paris airports are all practical for this tour. There is said to be a regular bus service from Deauville airport to the town, 8km distant, but details are hard to come by. There is a shuttle bus service from Beauvais to the centre of Paris and there are good transport links from the Paris airports to the city centre. There is a bus service from Deauville to Le Havre, operated by *Busverts Calvados*, www.busverts.fr. Le Havre and Harfleur can both be reached by rail from Paris and Deauville (Trouville-Deauville).

Where to Stay and Where to Eat
The websites listed below give information on local accommodation and restaurants for this tour:

www.lehavretourisme.com
www.normandy-tourism.org (in English) and www.normandie-tourisme.fr

Le Havre and Harfleur both have numerous bars and cafés.

Tour Two
Harfleur to Abbeville

This tour covers the itinerary from Henry's departure from Harfleur on 8 October 1415 until his arrival in the vicinity of the ford across the Somme at Blanchetaque five days later. The tour finishes at Abbeville and covers a distance of 160km.

What Happened
What Next from Henry?
In the English camp Henry had to decide what to do now that he had taken Harfleur. To secure his gains so far, he had made arrangements to repair and garrison Harfleur and to turn it into an English town. This was followed by a personal challenge to the dauphin. Henry's proposal was that the challenge would resolve his claims in France, with the proviso that Charles VI, twenty years Henry's senior, should continue to reign for the rest of his days with the crown passing to Henry on the death of the French king. Henry also proposed to wait at Harfleur for eight days to give the dauphin the chance to respond. The dauphin could not accept the challenge, but equally he could not refuse it. His only option was to ignore it. However, since the challenge was delivered by both English and French envoys, he could not avoid the challenge becoming known to the court and beyond. Henry could not have expected the dauphin to do otherwise than decline to reply, but he had secured a propaganda victory and given himself some thinking time while the eight days given for a reply elapsed.

It may be that Henry considered moving on to Dieppe (Point 10), Rouen and eventually Paris. In the event he decided to move off towards Calais. Since he left his artillery, gunners and carpenters behind in Harfleur it can be assumed that he had elected not to besiege any towns en route. Similarly, since he marched directly towards Calais, almost certainly intending to cross the Somme at the ford of Blanchetaque (Point 15) as used by Edward III immediately before the Battle of Crécy,

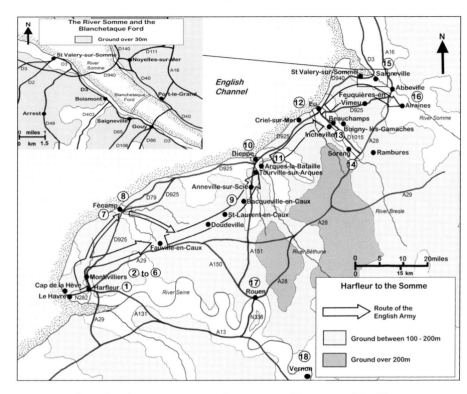

it is clear that he meant to get there as quickly as possible. The route also suggests that he was not seeking battle with the French. If that had been his objective, then he would surely have headed towards Rouen, where, as he must have known, the French army was gathering. Henry could at this stage have returned to England from Harfleur. To do so, however, would have risked all that he had gained. If he marched towards Calais, he could draw off the French forces from the vicinity of Harfleur while its fortifications were repaired and arrangements for the town's defence put in order. By doing so he would also keep the initiative and could impress the French with a show of strength. There was also a practical difficulty with returning directly from Harfleur. The shipping from Holland and Zealand used for the invasion had long since returned home. There were enough ships to return the sick to England from Normandy, but too few to move the whole army; such a move would have had to wait for the lengthy process of hiring and pressing ships to take its course.

The army that Henry now had at his disposal was somewhat diminished compared with the 12,000 combatants who had landed in August. Some 300 men-at-arms and 900 archers were left to garrison Harfleur, together with the gunners and carpenters. There had been some desertions, and a small number of troops had died during the siege either as a result of hostile action or from the dysentery that had struck the English camps. The number of deaths due to dysentery was small, but the disease had had a significant impact on Henry's fighting strength, since more than 1,300 combatants were unable to continue to serve and had to be repatriated. The decision to repatriate the sick was a prudent military decision. Taking the sick with him would have encumbered and slowed Henry's army. He would make better progress, and be better placed to fight, if he took only the fit. A number of replacements for the sick and dead had arrived, and in total the size of the army available to Henry for his onward march was probably between 8,000 and 9,000. Of these over 7,000 were archers. Although he had 25 per cent fewer men than when he arrived in France, this was still a good-sized army for the period.

The French

While Henry prepared to move towards Calais and the French army was assembling at Rouen (Point 17), the dauphin seemed to be in no hurry to move to the city, even after the surrender of Harfleur, and he was still 60km south-east of Rouen at Vernon (Point 18) when the king joined him on 7 October. They moved on together about 9 October and reached Rouen by 12 October. This slow progress was not due to a lack of a sense of urgency. Rather it indicated a concern that after Harfleur Henry V might turn his attention to Rouen. It would have been a disaster if Henry had laid siege to Rouen and trapped the king and the dauphin inside the city, and so it was prudent to wait and see what Henry did next. The news that Henry had decided to move towards the Somme and not Rouen probably reached the king and the dauphin around 9 October, and it was then safe for them to move from Vernon.

By the time Harfleur finally surrendered, the French army was probably 6,000 or so strong, and when Henry left the town the French troops started to move towards the Somme. Indeed, some at least of those who had been with the dauphin in Vernon moved to position themselves north of the river as he left for Rouen. Some contingents continued to gather at Rouen during October, including those of the Dukes of Bourbon and Anjou. The Duke of Orléans probably did not join the king at Rouen, but made directly for the bulk of the French army, which had already deployed to the north with the aim of intercepting Henry. Only a small contingent under the Duke of Bourbon seems to have moved from Rouen to join the main army.

Absent from the massing French forces was the Duke of Burgundy. At the beginning of September the royal princes had each been asked to bring 500 men-at-arms and 300 archers to the king's aid. However, there were continuing concerns about the loyalty of the Duke of Burgundy, and the request sent to the duke had acquainted him with decisions taken by the king's council, which confirmed the restoration of his honour and brought some relaxation to the terms concerning pardons for his supporters. The sting in the tail was that the Duke of Burgundy was asked not to come in person to join the assembling army. This probably reflected not only doubts about Burgundy's loyalty but also a desire to keep him apart from the Duke of Orléans to avoid the risk of reopening old quarrels. The Duke of Burgundy, not surprisingly, took offence at this request and also at the size of the contingent required, which he considered to be far too small for the job in hand. In the interests of an even-handed approach, it appears that the Duke of Orléans may also have been asked to stay away in person. In that case he either ignored the request or there was later a change of heart, which could explain why he did not make the rendezvous at Rouen but moved directly to join the army in the region of the Somme. Whatever the feelings of the Duke of Burgundy he did nevertheless mobilize his contingent. He also, however, assembled forces to defend his territory in the vicinity of Arras, and issued instructions to local lords to hold themselves ready to join his contingent rather than to respond to the summons to join the king and the dauphin. With doubts over the Duke of Burgundy's loyalty the king left troops in Paris to defend the city. In addition to royal concerns over the duke's conduct, there seems to have been a less than complete response in some areas to the initial proclamation to mobilize. Around 20 September the *bailli* of Amiens was instructed to repeat the proclamation and orders were also issued for towns to provide artillery and other equipment in support of the army.

To add to the French worries, Duke John of Brittany had entered into a truce with Henry V in 1414, and, shortly after the start of the siege of

Harfleur, Henry had sent an envoy to remind the Duke of Brittany of his obligations. The French king had, nonetheless, called on the duke to provide support. Presented with this dilemma of his obligations to both kings, the Duke of Brittany made haste slowly. He did raise his company, but had only reached Falaise, 110km to the west, by the time Harfleur fell and he remained there for eight days before moving on to Rouen. His onward progress remained slow, and by the date of the battle he had only reached Amiens. In sum, King Charles VI and the dauphin were presented with considerable political difficulties that compounded the logistical challenges of raising and deploying an army to confront Henry. Of these, the logistics had been the over-riding factor in preventing mobilization in time to save Harfleur, but despite these difficulties and the political complications, a considerable army was gathered subsequently to harass Henry's march towards Calais and to confront him at Agincourt.

The March to the Somme

Henry left Harfleur (Point 1) on 8 October, with his route initially taking him to the west of Montivilliers (Points 2 to 6). His departure and direction of march would not have come as a surprise to the French, since news of his intent to march to Calais had reached Boulogne two days before. Montivilliers is about 4km north of Harfleur on the river Lézarde. It was a good-sized town and was garrisoned by several companies of French troops under Sir Louis de Lignières, Pierre Hotot and Colart de Villequier with a company of Genoese crossbowmen.

It is, perhaps, testament to the fortifications of Montivilliers (Point 2) that, although it was so close to Harfleur, Henry had made no attempt to take the town. It was defended by 8m-high stone walls, built in the fourteenth century, around a perimeter of 1.5km, and the walls were surrounded by a ditch 30m wide and 10–12m deep. There were three main gates, four postern gates used to facilitate movement for townspeople in times of peace, secondary gates and eighteen interval towers.

The English army would probably have skirted close to Montivilliers, although keeping out of bow shot, over the ground now occupied by the urban sprawl to the west of the town. This would have avoided having to climb the relatively steep slopes further to the west and would have given easier access to the higher ground and the onward north-easterly

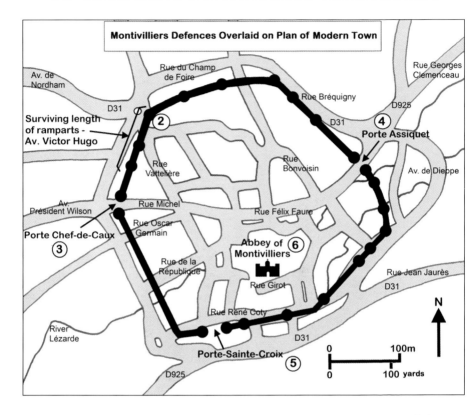

route towards the plateau of the Pays-de-Caux. However, the English faced a significant threat from the garrison as they passed, and it seems that Henry sent out a force to screen his army from attacks. Nevertheless, there was a sortie from the town and a number of English troops were taken prisoner and killed.

The Army on the March

It is difficult to visualize a medieval army on the march, but in the First World War a British army division of twenty thousand men with five thousand or so horses stretched over 25km of road and took seven hours to pass a point. Given the poor roads of the fifteenth century Henry's army would probably have moved on a broad front rather than in a column, but nevertheless managing a large army on the move was a considerable enterprise. According to a contemporary account, Henry had ordered his men to carry rations for eight days. If this was intended to be sufficient for the march to Calais, it implies either an underestimate of the distance or an overly optimistic assessment of the speed the army could make – or a combination of both. The average speed the army achieved, around 23km per day, was reasonable for the period. However, even if he had been able to march directly to Calais at this speed without hindrance, a distance of at least 270km, his army would have faced a march of around twelve days. In the event, due to the longer route he was compelled to take and the speed of march he could achieve, he took seventeen days to arrive at Maisoncelle on the eve of battle and a total of twenty-two days to get to Calais. Thus, eight days' rations would have been insufficient for the march to Calais, and Henry was exposing his army to the risk of food shortages from the outset. However, a dispersed marching order would have facilitated foraging from the countryside to supplement the rations carried by the troops. It may be that, rather than a miscalculation on Henry's part, the eight days' supplies were intended as a contingency to supplement the forage which an army on the march in the period would expect to gather as it advanced.

When Henry V set off from Harfleur he had an army of between eight and nine thousand men. On top of this he would probably have had several thousand non-combatants, including pages and men drawn from many medieval trades. Feeding an army of this size would be a huge task, and the daily demand would be for 15 tonnes or more of food. An even bigger challenge would be feeding and watering the horses. There could well have been twenty thousand horses, and their daily needs for food and water were very considerable. Each horse would need about 25kg of fresh grass or 10kg of dry fodder per day. In view of the quantities required, it would not be practical to carry dry fodder, so each day some 200 tonnes of dry fodder or several hectares of pasture would have to be found. The water requirements were also demanding since each horse would drink around 18 litres a day. Since Henry V was on the move in October, village store houses could be expected to have been replenished from the summer's harvest, and raiding villages would provide some of the needs of the army. Towns were also persuaded to give supplies of food in return for their safety from destruction. However, French detachments would certainly have harassed foraging parties and villagers would have done their best to hide animals and supplies, and as the march progressed the army became increasingly short of food.

There was concern in Fécamp (Points 7 and 8), on the coast 30km north of Montivilliers, about the threat posed by the English on their departure from Harfleur. In view of their experience only five years before when an English naval squadron had attacked the town, leaving it ruined and deserted apart from the abbey, it is not surprising that some of the population had fled in fear lest Henry should turn his attention to their town after Harfleur. Conscious of the threat, Abbot Estod, brother of the Sire d'Estouteville who was defending Harfleur, raised a militia for the defence of the town, comprising townsmen, people from the surrounding countryside and inhabitants of the abbey, to reinforce some men-at-arms garrisoned in the town.

According to tradition Henry's army bombarded Fécamp. However, not only had the artillery been left behind at Harfleur, but a route along the coast would not have made sense since numerous rivers run into the sea along this coast through deep, steep-sided valleys that would have slowed the progress of the army. The inland route through the Pays-de-Caux would have been much more practicable. Thus it is unlikely that there was a serious assault on Fécamp. Nevertheless, one man-at-arms and two archers were taken prisoner near the town. They were probably members of a scouting or foraging party, and there is an account of the abbey being compelled to contribute food or money to the English troops. In reprisal for the role of the abbot, the abbey's lands in England were seized.

Once beyond Montivilliers, Henry's first halt is said to have been at Fauville-en-Caux on the plateau of the Pays-de-Caux. The detailed route from Fauville to the next known town on the itinerary, Arques-la-Bataille (Point 11), is unknown, but it is likely that the main axis of march would have been through Doudeville, St-Laurent-en-Caux, Bacqueville-en-Caux (Point 9), Anneville-sur-Scie and Tourville-sur-Arques. Once on the plateau of the Pays-de-Caux, the going becomes easy across a wide open plain, punctuated by a few minor valleys. Further north the escarpments to the east of the rivers are steep, but along the likely route the river crossings would not have presented any difficulties.

Bacqueville had had a castle from the eleventh century, surrounded by a curtain wall with nine towers, a water-filled moat and a drawbridge. The castle was not attacked in 1415, but it was surrendered to the English in January 1419 after the fall of Rouen and all the occupants were allowed to leave with safe conducts. The Sire de Bacqueville, Guillaume VIII Martel, entrusted by the king as the bearer of the *oriflamme* the previous month, was to die at Agincourt, along with his son-in-law John III Martel, the Seneschal of Eu, two brothers-in-law and a cousin.

Arques, now known as Arques-la-Bataille in commemoration of a sixteenth-century battle fought by another Henry (Henry IV of France, during the French Wars of Religion), was reached on 11 October. The town was not fortified, but it was defended by a large and important castle, originally built in the eleventh century, standing in a strong position on a tongue of high ground to the south of the town and surrounded by deep ditches dug into the rock. General improvements had been made by King Charles V in 1367, and the importance of the castle at Arques had been recognized by him in 1390 when he had given orders that guard was to be mounted day and night, despite a general exemption relaxing this duty for towns and castles away from the coast. In 1399 Coulart d'Estouteville, another member of the family which had played a role in the defence of Harfleur and Fécamp, complained that taxes for the upkeep of the castle had been unpaid for fourteen years. King Charles VI authorized the collection of the arrears to enable Coulart to repair the defences. However, although Coulart was still captain of the castle, it was not in a fully defensive condition in 1415. The townspeople had attempted to improve their defences by blocking access to the town with felled trees and other obstacles, but with a weakened castle the inhabitants and the garrison would not have been able to resist an attack by Henry. However, although he drew up his troops in view of the castle and the garrison responded by firing guns, Henry did not wish to squander resources and time assaulting such towns and fortresses. There were no casualties from the artillery fire, and Henry negotiated a safe passage and victuals in return for sparing the town and the surrounding area from burning and looting.

In view of the route across the Pays-de-Caux, it is likely that the approach to the castle was from the south along the spur of ground on which it sits. The rivers Béthune and Varenne flow below the castle to the east out to the sea at Dieppe. At their confluence just beyond Arques-la-Bataille they become the river Arques. They share a flood plain, about 1.5km wide, which is the north-eastern boundary of the Pays-de-Caux.

The rivers would not have presented a serious challenge to Henry's army. However, the flood plain has relatively steep hills rising to about 100m on both sides, and it is possible that the crossing was made about 5km south-east of Arques-la-Bataille, where re-entrants with gentle gradients on both sides of the rivers would have allowed easy entry to and exit from the flood plain. On the eastern side the exit would approximately follow the route of the modern D149. This would also offer an easier crossing of the river Eaulne without the need to pass through the extensive forest to the east of the town.

The French had been concerned that Henry would attack Dieppe, only 8km north-west of Arques and had garrisoned the town. However, since Henry's goal was to reach Calais rather than seize further towns, from Arques he set off towards Eu (Point 12) on 12 October. Once across the river Eaulne beyond Arques the going is easy again with gently undulating terrain until approaching the river Yères near Criel-sur-Mer about 10km before reaching Eu. The river itself would not have been a serious obstacle. However, the escarpments on both sides are steep, and to the east the ground rises some 100m above the river. The route of the modern D22 would have provided gentle gradients into and out of the valley. Overall it would have been a hard day's march, and it may be that the bulk of the army moved directly towards crossings of the Bresle, perhaps bivouacking short of the river, with only a detachment moving to the town. Eu was walled, with a castle and an abbey on a steep hill to the south of the river Bresle. In 1415 it was held by Charles d'Artois, who may have left the gathering French army to return to the town to assist in its defence. If so, he subsequently returned to the army and was captured at Agincourt. When the English approached with banners flying, the French made a sortie, variously reported as being by the townsmen on foot or by mounted troops, which resulted in casualties on both sides. Among the French casualties was Lancelot Pierre, who, although mortally wounded by a lance, killed his English assailant. As with other towns on the route, Henry had no intention of attacking Eu. However, with a crossing to be made of the Bresle near the town he needed to be sure that the garrison did not pose a threat. From the French side, they could not have resisted a determined assault by an army of the size of Henry's. Thus a compromise was reached whereby, in return for the delivery of food to the army, the town and the surrounding countryside were spared.

Confirmation that Henry had left Harfleur reached Boulogne on 11 October, when the English were in the vicinity of Arques. The messenger also reported that Henry was heading for the ford across the Somme at Blanchetaque. By 12 October d'Albret, the Constable of France, had moved to Abbeville (Point 16), on the other side of the Somme from Henry, intending to block any English attempt to cross the river. At about this time, possibly during the engagement outside Eu, the English took some prisoners. From these men they learnt that the French army was gathering with a view to giving battle at Henry's crossing of the Somme. It is possible that Eu had been garrisoned to slow down the advance of the English and buy the constable time to secure Blanchetaque. Similarly, one of the French marshals, Boucicaut, may have been operating out on the right of Henry's army, harrying foraging and scouting parties to slow the advance to the Somme.

Henry's crossing of the Bresle was probably between the villages of Beauchamps and Incheville. Indeed, one report talks of the army crossing at the small settlement of Gousseauville in the commune of

The Bresle valley above the crossing at Gousseauville, looking back in the direction from which the army had come, showing the descent into the river and the climb out to gain the easier plains beyond towards the Somme. The river runs in the background behind the lakes. (Peter Hoskins)

Wide, open land on the approach to the Somme. (Peter Hoskins)

Incheville (Point 13), just over 1.5km south-east of the village. This makes sense since, although the river itself would not have been a serious obstacle, the river valley, about 1.5km wide, once again has steep hills on both sides, but near Incheville the gradients are less marked than further north-west towards Eu. As with earlier crossings, modern roads, this time the D58 into Incheville and the D2 beyond the river, follow relatively easy routes into and out of the valley. Boucicaut is said to have crossed the river about 8km further upstream near Soreng (Point 14) and there was probably a skirmish between elements of the two armies near Buigny-lès-Gamaches.

On the higher ground beyond the Bresle the going is easy once again, with wide, open views until the land slowly descends towards the valley of the Somme. There are steep slopes to the escarpment on the approach to the Somme, but a number of valleys allow an easy descent, including the route of the D403 to Boismont, which was used by Canadian troops on their advance to the Somme in 1944. On Sunday, 13 October Henry continued his march towards the river with the intention of crossing it the next day. There are accounts of the army either passing close to St-Valery-sur-Somme, which suggests a route close to the modern D940, or through the area known as the Vimeu, which implies a more inland route directly towards Blanchetaque. It became apparent to Henry that the French had broken the causeways and bridges and were gathered in strength on the far side of the river. In 1346 Henry's great-grandfather Edward III had forced a crossing of the Somme at Blanchetaque. However, with an army perhaps 14,000 strong he had had many more men than Henry and, although he may have been opposed by as many as 3,000 men, probably only some 500 of them were men-at-arms. Henry had heard that there may have been 6,000 French troops arrayed to counter his passage of the ford. Although Henry's army was more numerous than the opposition, it would have been vulnerable during the crossing, and it is not surprising that he turned away from Blanchetaque and headed upstream along the bank of the Somme.

There are several explanations why the ford of Blanchetaque, a corruption of the French for a white stain, was so called; the two reasons most widely quoted are either that the name was derived from the causeway being made of white chalk, or that there was a white chalk mark on the northern bank of the river used as a reference point to guide those crossing the river. An eighteenth-century map shows the name running down the centre of the river close to the estuary. The river has changed a great deal over the centuries, with construction of a canal and a railway and reclamation of land. Consequently, it is difficult to visualize what Henry's army would have faced. However, having descended to the river from the higher ground, the flood plain would have been a little over 3km wide before the ground started to rise again on the far side. Even if not all of this stretch was under water at low tide, there would have been extensive marshland adjacent to the river. Even today, with the water controlled by the modern works, the marshy nature of the area is evident and many of the tracks are built on low, elevated causeways. The medieval causeway is said to have been wide enough for twelve men abreast. It is possible that there was a central causeway constructed of chalk to support wheeled vehicles with a wider area passable by horses and those on foot. Abbeville was a port in the Middle Ages, and the water level at high tide would have been sufficient to allow the passage of ships. Although we cannot be sure precisely

Looking back across Blanchetaque from close to the Chalet de la Gué de Blanche Taque towards the higher ground near Saigneville. (Peter Hoskins)

where the ford of Blanchetaque was located, it was probably between Noyelles-sur-Mer and Saigneville. An eighteenth-century map shows a ford running across the mouth of the river from La Ferté, now a suburb of St-Valery-sur-Somme, to Le Crotoy, and this has been proposed as an alternative location. However, the weight of current opinion favours the Saigneville option, and there is a place marked on the 1:25,000 scale map called the Chalet et Gué de Blanche Taque, or the chalet and ford of Blanche Taque, much where the ford could be expected to be. The chalet, once a hunting lodge and now used as offices for management of the conservation of the Somme Bay wetlands, is a distinctive landmark. From this position a good impression can be gained of the width of the flood plain of the Somme, and a little exploration on foot shows the marshy nature of the land.

The Route by Car
From Harfleur (Point 1) take the D925 to Montivilliers (Points 2 to 6). The route to Fauville-en-Caux from Montivilliers is initially on the D925

and then the D31 and D39 to St-Romain-de-Colbosc. From here follow the N15/D6015 to Lanquetot and then the D109 to the village of Fauville. Fécamp (Points 7 and 8) can be visited by taking the D925 from Montivilliers, and the route rejoined at Fauville by following the D926. From Fauville follow the D149 through Doudeville and St-Laurent-en-Caux to Bacqueville-en-Caux (Point 9), and then the D23, N27, D3 and D23 through Anneville-sur-Scie to Tourville-sur-Arques. Take the D927 into Dieppe (Point 10). From Dieppe follow the D154 to Arques-la-Bataille (Point 11). Continue on the D154 to the intersection with the D925 and follow this road to Eu (Point 12).

To visit the potential crossing points of the river Bresle by the French and English armies and the village of Buigny-lès-Gamaches, follow the D49 from Eu to Incheville (Point 13) and on to Soreng (Point 14) in the commune of Monchaux-Soreng. Return to Incheville on the D49, cross the river to Beauchamps and take an unnumbered road to Embreville and then the D190 to Buigny. To see Blanchetaque (Point 15) take an unnumbered road from Buigny and then follow the D48 through Feuquières-en-Vimeu to the D925. Follow this road towards Abbeville (Point 16). At Miannay take the D86 to Cahon. Then follow minor, unnumbered roads, initially the Chemin du Long Rideau to Gouy and then the Chemin du Canal, cross the canal to Petit Port and continue to the intersection with the D40. Turn left and continue to Port-le-Grand. In the village, turn left by the railway halt (the road to the right is Rue Pascal), cross the railway and turn right to continue on the Chemin de Valois. Take the third turning to the left after about 2km. The turning is signposted Station Biologique de Blanchetaque et Ferme des Bouchers. To complete the tour, return to Petit Port and take the D40 to Abbeville.

The Route on Foot and by Bike

The walking and cycling route is generally through open country predominantly along minor roads but with some paths and tracks. The walking is easy going with occasional climbs and descents of around 100m. The overall distance is 162km.

Leaving Harfleur (Point 1), follow the Rue du Moulin, off the Avenue de la République, and then paths towards the D6015, across the Impasse de la Forge to join the *GR2* way-marked path which passes under the major roads to join the *GR2 Variante*. Follow this path and then the *GR21* into the centre of Montivilliers (Points 2 to 6).

> *Some parts of the route between Harfleur and Montivilliers are on natural surfaces and are steep in places. An alternative route for cyclists is along the D925 to Montivilliers.*

From Montivilliers follow the D925 to Epouville and then the D52 through Angerville-l'Orcher and Manneville-la-Goupil. About 400m beyond Manneville-le-Goupil, just after the intersection with the D252, turn right onto an unnumbered road to Bréauté. Leave Bréauté on the D452 and follow this road to St-Maclou-la-Brière. Follow the D104 to the intersection with the D17, turn right and take this road for about 300m. Turn left onto an unnumbered road through Hattenville to join the D149 for 1km into Fauville-en-Caux. (Note: the map shows an unnumbered road as a continuation of the D104 at the intersection with the D17, passing through Equimbosc and avoiding the short stretch on the D17. This road is blocked at a farm after about 600m and is not passable.)

Leave Fauville-en-Caux on the D149, and 400m after crossing the D926 fork right onto the D228. Approximately 1km after leaving St-Pierre-Levis, turn right onto an unnumbered road past Rucquemare, and then follow the D29 to Envronville. Turn right onto the D5 and then immediately left onto an unnumbered road to Ferme du Bois Hébert. The road joins the *GR211* footpath near the farm. The path can be followed to Rocquefort, but it is shorter and more straightforward to stay on the unnumbered road and by-pass the village. An unnumbered road comes in from the left, and after about 150m fork left, again on an unnumbered road, through le Grand Tot to Hautot-St-Sulpice. Now follow the D110 to Doudeville.

> *A section of the GR211 near Rocquefort, on the route between Cauville-en-Caux and Doudeville, is on a natural surface of grass and earth. An alternative route is to stay on the unnumbered road to by-pass Rocquefort to the south.*

From Doudeville take the D149 for about 1.5km, and then turn left onto an unnumbered road. Take the first right after about 300m. Continue through the hamlets of Colmont and Boucourt and turn left onto the D89. Turn right at the junction with the D25 and follow this road and the D149 through St-Laurent-en-Caux to Bacqueville-en-

Caux (Point 9). An alternative route, which passes the current chateau and possible site of the medieval castle, is to turn right off the D149 about 1.5km beyond Royville to follow the *GR212A* footpath past Beautot to Bacqueville-en-Caux.

Leave Bacqueville-en-Caux on the D23 and after about 3km turn left to follow the D55 to the outskirts of Offranville. Follow the D54 to St-Aubin-sur-Scie, and turn left onto the N27 for about 500m. Turn right at la Vieille Côte onto a minor track, le Chemin de la Messé, and follow this and subsequent minor roads through the hamlets of le Beau Site and Calmont to Arques-la-Bataille (Point 11). The castle is signposted and is about 500m south of the town centre.

From Arques-la-Bataille follow the D54 and then the D56 after crossing the D1. After approximately 2.5km, turn left onto the forest road, Route des Quatre Quartiers, leading into the Fôret d'Arques. About 400m after the crossroads, the Rond des Quatre Quartiers, the road joins a way-marked *GRP* footpath. Follow the path out of the forest to Sauchay-le-Bas. Turn right on to the D928 for 500m and then turn left onto an unnumbered road to join the D454 near the farm les Rendus. There is an alternative route from the Rond des Quatres Quartiers which saves some distance but involves a scramble of about 200m down a steep wooded slope: take the Route de Rouval and when this runs out continue straight on down the slope to join the Route de Sauchay. This alternative route joins the *GRP* at Hocquélus farm.

> The alternative route through the Fôret d'Arques via the Route de Rouval is unsuitable for cycles. The primary route from the Rond des Quatre Quartiers is initially on a good, packed stone surface for about 800m, but it then becomes a grass surface, rutted and with pot holes, descending quite steeply towards Ancourt. It is muddy and slippery when wet. An alternative route for cyclists is to remain on the D56 from Arques-la-Bataille to St-Nicolas-d'Aliermont, and then follow the D256 to Intraville. Take the D222 to join the D354 and the main route about 2km north-east of Tourville-la-Chapelle.

Once on the D454 continue through Glicourt and Tourville-la-Chapelle to join the D222. Follow the D222 to Guilmécourt and then take the D454. About 150m before the intersection with the D226 leave the road to the right to join a *GRP* footpath. This path is on a paved surface and follows the course of a disused railway until just short of Eu (Point 12). The footpath then follows the D49 into the town.

From the centre of Eu, in the Place Guillaume le Conquérant, take the Rue de l'Hospice, and turn right into Rue de la Teinturerie. Cross the D925c and follow unnumbered roads to join the D1015 in Ponts-et-Marais. Turn right to follow this road and take the second turn to the left in Oust-Marest onto an unnumbered road. After 100m turn right to follow the *GRP des Forêts de Haute Normandie* to join an unnumbered road 1km west of Méneslies.

> *The latter part of the section of the GRP des Forêts de Haute Normandie after Oust-Marest is across fields. Cyclists should continue on the unnumbered road through Méneslies after leaving the D1015.*

Continue on the unnumbered road through Méneslies to Woincourt and then follow the D1925 to Feuquières-en-Vimeu. In Feuquières-en-Vimeu turn left onto an unnumbered road at the eastern end of the central square. Follow this road through Franleu, join the D106 to Boubert and follow the D403 to Boismont. Turn left onto the D3 and after about 200m turn right onto an unnumbered road. After 1km the road turns sharply right to cross the canal from Abbeville to St-Valery. Continue on this road until the junction with a road that runs parallel to the railway embankment; turn right onto this road and continue for 2.5km. A short distance down the road on the right, the Chemin de Blanchetaque, is the Chalet de Blanchetaque (Point 15). From Blanchetaque return to the road parallel to the railway and continue to Port-le-Grand. Follow the D40 and turn right onto the D86. Cross the canal and turn left to follow the towpath on the southern bank into Abbeville (Point 16). (Note: the map shows a number of paths in the stretch of flood plain between Boismont and Port-le-Grand which seem to offer a shorter route than the one described here. Some of these are impracticable and others are private and not accessible. Attempting to follow them is likely to result in a longer walk than planned!)

What to See
Harfleur
Point 1: See Tour 1, Points 6 to 13, pages 52–57, and plan of Harfleur, page 41.

Montivilliers

Point 2: There are remains of the fortifications in the Avenue Victor Hugo (GPS 49.546633, 0.189042), with a section of wall and remains of towers, including the interval tower Tourelle Vatellière, at the junction with Rue Vatellière. The line of the walls can be traced close to the modern street pattern from the roundabout in the north-west of the town (GPS 49.547221, 0.189112) to the east of Avenue Victor Hugo, across Rue Michel, to the east of the Rue de la Commune 1871, east along the Rue René Coty, north-east along the Rue des Remparts Châtel, west of the Rue de la Barbacane, across Rue du Faubourg Assiquet, along Rue Bréquiqny, and then west to the south of the Champ de Foire along the Impasse des Remparts.

The interval tower, Tourelle Valletière, at the junction of the Rue Valletière and Avenue Victor Hugo. (Peter Hoskins)

A surviving stretch of the town wall in Avenue Victor Hugo. (Peter Hoskins)

Points 3, 4 and 5: The three gates no longer exist, but the Porte Chef-de-Caux was located on Rue Michel, close to the Place Commandant O'Reilly (GPS 49.545655, 0.188372), the Porte Assiquet on Rue Assiquet south-west of the Place des Combattants (GPS 49.546782, 0.195616), and the Porte Ste-Croix on Rue René Coty (GPS 49.543698, 0.191054).

Point 6: Montivilliers Abbey was founded for women in the seventh century. It was destroyed by the Vikings but reconstructed from the eleventh century. The Hundred Years War lay heavily on the abbey. Revenues from lands held in England had dried up late in the fourteenth century and the population of twenty-eight nuns early in the fifteenth century was less than half the strength set out by statute. No doubt the abbess, Isabelle de Boscherville, who had decided to stay put, was relieved that the English passed by the town in 1415. However, late in the following year or early in 1417 she decided that the prospect

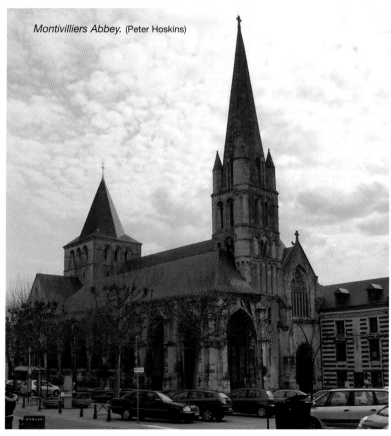

Montivilliers Abbey. (Peter Hoskins)

of another English invasion was too much to bear and she fled to Rouen with the majority of her nuns. The abbey church, in Place François Mitterand (GPS 49.545094, 0.19225), and other abbey buildings survive, including the eleventh-century chapter house and a dormitory and refectory dating from the thirteenth century: www.abbaye-montivilliers.fr.

Fécamp
Fécamp was not on the main line of march, but English prisoners, probably members of a scouting or foraging party, were taken near the town.

Point 7: The ruins of the castle of Fécamp can be found in the centre of the town in the Place du Général Leclerc (GPS 49.755032, 0.38031). Sir John Fastolf became captain of the castle on its surrender to the English in 1419. Opposite the castle is the abbey of the Holy Trinity. There has been an abbey on the site since the seventh century, but the current buildings are much later, with only some minor vestiges from the medieval period.

The castle, or more properly the Ducal Palace, in Frévent. The first stone castle was built in the tenth century. Construction continued under subsequent Dukes of Normandy, and parts of the remains were built by King Henry II of England at the end of the twelfth century. (Peter Hoskins)

The Chapelle du Nôtre Dame du Salut.
(Peter Hoskins)

Point 8: On high ground to the east of the town in Bourg-Baudouin stands the Chapelle de Notre-Dame du Salut (GPS 49.767019, 0.371384). According to legend this was one of three chapels constructed by Robert I, Duke of Normandy, in thanks for his escape from a shipwreck. The current chapel was built in the thirteenth century. In 1419 Bourg-Baudouin passed into the hands of Sir John Fastolf, who had taken part in the siege of Harfleur. He had been invalided home at the end of the siege, but had returned to join the garrison and in early 1416 had been granted the lordship and manor of Frileuse, now absorbed in the agglomeration of Le Havre. On taking possession of Bourg-Baudouin he also became captain of the castle of Fécamp on its surrender to the English in 1419.

Bacqueville-en-Caux
Point 9: Bacqueville, whose lord had been appointed to carry the *oriflamme*, was probably on the English line of advance towards the Somme. There was a castle here in the fifteenth century. It was taken

by the Burgundians in 1418, handed over to the English and given to John Lord Roos, who had been with Henry in 1415, the following year. The castle was razed in 1764 and some of the stone used to build the current chateau. The castle's location is uncertain, but it is thought to have stood to the west of the sixteenth-century church, seriously damaged in 1940 and subsequently reconstructed, on the hill above the current chateau (GPS 49.785448, 0.993834). There is a thirteenth-century cross, the cross of St Léonard, 1km north of the village on the D123 (GPS 49.79714, 0.996316).

The cross of St Léonard in Bacqueville-en-Caux. According to a local belief, tying a ribbon around the cross will help children to walk. Even today the cross attracts numerous ribbons. (Peter Hoskins)

Dieppe

Point 10: The French garrisoned Dieppe to counter an anticipated threat by the English, although in the event Henry's forces did not approach the town. The castle in Rue des Chastes (GPS 49.924538, 1.070736) was originally built in the twelfth century but destroyed in 1195. It was restored in the fourteenth century and in 1360 was integrated within the fortifications built to defend the town. The large west tower is thought to date from the fourteenth century. The castle fell into English hands in 1420 and was recaptured by the French in 1435.

Arques-la-Bataille

Point 11: Henry drew up his men in front of the castle, but went on his way peacefully in exchange for safe passage and victuals. The castle stands on high ground to the south of the town (GPS 49.878168, 1.125906). It was originally

The castle in Dieppe, garrisoned in anticipation of Henry's passage. (Peter Hoskins)

built in the eleventh century with a single gate to the north. It has undergone numerous changes over the centuries, and the first gate seen as the visitor approaches from the town is a gate built when a roughly quadrangular bastion was added in the late fifteenth century. The original gate was a little further back, but the general line of the main ramparts with this second, now interior, gate on the north side is thought to follow that of the original fortress. The keep in the south-west corner is typical of the twelfth century and a second entrance on the south side, protected by a drawbridge, was built in the reign of King Charles V, possibly as part of general improvements he made in 1367. An unusual feature of the castle is the ditch dug into the rock, which may date from the original construction of the castle, around 20m wide and 15m deep. It may have been surmounted by a wooden palisade to provide a first line of defence. The well to supply water to the garrison was over 100m deep. The castle was taken by the English in 1419 and remained in their possession for thirty years before its surrender by the Duke of Somerset in 1449. Joan of Arc was briefly held here in 1430 on the way to her trial at Rouen. The castle suffered considerable damage in 1944 when retreating German troops destroyed munitions stored

The eastern side of Arques castle; stretching away to the keep at the southern end are the ramparts and the deep, dry ditch. (Peter Hoskins)

The keep at the southern end of Arques castle. (Peter Hoskins)

within its confines. In 2013 it was closed to the public pending repairs. However, a good impression of the castle can be gained by walking around the external perimeter.

Eu

Point 12: There was a skirmish between English and French soldiers as Henry's army passed Eu. However, the town and the surrounding area were spared attack in return for supplies of food. The castle in the town had had an important place in Norman history, having been the site of William the Conqueror's betrothal to Matilda in 1049. The castle was another lodging place for Joan of Arc for one night in 1430 on the way to her trial in Rouen. The medieval castle has not survived, but the collegiate church of St Laurent (GPS 50.048542, 1.419951), Place Guillaume le Conquérant, remains. The church is named after St Lawrence O'Toole, Archbishop of Dublin, who died here in 1181 on his way to meet King Henry II of England. Originally built in the eleventh century, it suffered fire damage twice in the fifteenth century.

The church of St Laurent in Eu. (Peter Hoskins)

The river Bresle at Gousseauville, looking back to the west, and the route down to the river taken by the English army. (Peter Hoskins)

Crossings of the Bresle

Point 13: Henry probably crossed the Bresle south-east of Eu between the villages of Beauchamps (GPS 50.017336, 1.507616) and Incheville (GPS 50.016068, 1.497145), possibly near the small settlement of Gousseauville (GPS 50.00156, 1.518002) in Incheville, just over 1.5km south-east of the village. The river in Gousseauville can be reached along Rue Madame de Sévigné.

Point 14: The possible French crossing of the Bresle is about 8km further upstream near Soreng. The western façade and the north wall of the church of St Martin, in Rue André Carpentier (GPS 49.95541, 1.585549), date from the twelfth century. The river Bresle can be reached along the nearby Rue Monthières (GPS 49.955866, 1.587147).

The church of St Martin in Soreng in the commune of Monchaux-Soreng.
(Peter Hoskins)

The Chalet de Blanchetaque. (Peter Hoskins)

Blanchetaque
Point 15: The eastern end of the approximate position of the old ford of
Blanchetaque where Henry V had hoped to cross the Somme is marked
by the Chalet de Blanche Taque (GPS 50.160103, 1.724893), formerly a
hunting lodge and now used as administrative offices for management
of the Somme estuary wetlands. The chalet has, of course, no historic
significance but it serves as a useful reference point to gain an
impression of the Somme valley near the ford.

Abbeville

Point 16: D'Albret, the Constable of France, positioned himself at Abbeville to block Henry's anticipated crossing of the Somme at Blanchetaque. The town suffered a great deal during both world wars, and in particular during the Second World War. Much of the town is post-war and drab and uninteresting, but the thirteenth-century belfry in Rue Gontier Patin (GPS 50.107166, 1.832962) survives.

The Abbeville Belfry.
(Peter Hoskins)

The keep of Rouen castle, now known as La Tour Jeanne d'Arc. (Peter Hoskins)

Further Afield

Away from the route but closely tied to events during the campaign are Rouen (Point 17) and Vernon (Point 18), both of which have a rich heritage of surviving medieval buildings. Among the many monuments to be seen in Rouen, where the French army had been summoned to assemble in response to Henry's invasion, are the cathedral in Place de la Cathédrale (GPS 49.440377, 1.09422), the site of Joan of Arc's execution in the Place du Vieux Marché (GPS 49.443052, 1.088396) and

La Tour des Archives in Vernon, formerly the keep of the castle. (Peter Hoskins)

the keep of the castle, La Tour Jeanne d'Arc, in Rue du Donjon (GPS 49.44647, 1.094393), where she was held during her trial. The Rouen tourism website has detailed information on museums and architectural monuments: www.rouentourisme.com.

At Vernon, where the dauphin waited during the siege of Harfleur, before moving on to Rouen with his father when it was safe to do so after Henry's departure en route to Calais, the medieval monuments include the collegial church of Notre Dame in Rue Carnot (GPS 49.093274, 1.485931), the twelfth-century castle keep, the Tour des Archives in Rue des Écuries des Gardes (GPS 49.093826,1.484151) and numerous domestic buildings, with Rue Potard (GPS 49.093956,1.484983) having fine examples of half-timbered buildings: see www.vernon27.fr/Decouvrir-Vernon.

Maps

Maps at 1:25,000, 1:50,000 and 1:100,000 Scales
Published by the *Institut National de l'Information Géographique et Forestière (IGN)* www.ign.fr

Cartes de Randonnée – 1:25,000		
1710ET – Le Havre	1910O – Yvetot	2107OT – Le Tréport
1810O – Bolbec	1909OT – St-Valery-en-Caux	2207O – Abbeville
1810E – Lillebonne	2008OT – Dieppe.EU	
Série Orange – 1:50,000		
M1711 – Le Havre	M1710 – Montivilliers	M1810 – Bolbec
M2208 – Dieppe Est	M1910 – Yvetot	M1909 – Doudeville
M2108 – Gamaches	M2207 – Abbeville	
TOP 100 – 1:100,000		
TOP100107 – Rouen/Le Havre		TOP100103 – Amiens/Arras

How to Get There and Back by Public Transport

Deauville, Beauvais, Lille and Paris airports are all practical for this tour. There is said to be a regular bus service from Deauville airport to the town, 8km distant, but details are hard to come by. There is a shuttle bus service from Beauvais to the centre of Paris and there are good transport links from the Paris airports to the city centre. Lille airport has a shuttle bus service to the railway stations in the city. There is a bus service from Deauville to Le Havre, operated by *Busverts Calvados*, www.busverts.fr. Le Havre, Harfleur and Abbeville can all be reached by rail from Paris and Deauville (Trouville-Deauville). A number of intermediate towns on the route also have railway stations.

Montivilliers, Doudeville and Arques-la-Bataille are within the *TER* Haute-Normandie region. Some services on the line through Doudeville are provided by buses; bicycles can only be carried on trains on this line. The service to Arques-la-Bataille is provided by buses only and bicycles cannot be carried. Eu is within the *TER* Picardie region.

Where to Stay and Where to Eat
The websites listed below give information on local accommodation and restaurants for this tour:

www.lehavretourisme.com
www.normandy-tourism.org (in English) and www.normandie-tourisme.fr
www.dieppetourisme.com
www.eu-tourisme.com
www.abbeville-tourisme.com
www.visit-somme.com (in English) and www.somme-tourisme.com

Cafés, bars and restaurants are few and far between in small villages on this tour. However, there are several places in each of the following towns: Harfleur, Montivilliers, Fécamp, Fauville-en-Caux, Doudeville, St-Laurent-en-Caux, Bacqueville-en-Caux, Dieppe, Arques-la-Bataille, Eu and Feuquières-en-Vimeu.

Tour Three
Abbeville to Péronne

Blanchetaque to the Crossing of the Somme – Béthencourt-sur-Somme

This tour covers the route from Henry V's decision not to attempt to force a crossing of the Somme at Blanchetaque around 13 October 1415 until his army halted for the night of 20 October in the vicinity of Athies and Monchy-Lagache after crossing the Somme to the south of Péronne on 19 October. The tour starts in Abbeville and finishes in Péronne, and covers a distance of 144km.

What happened
French Preparations
While the French king and the dauphin were arriving at Rouen on 12 October and joining elements of the army gathering in the city, Henry was well to the north-east approaching the Somme estuary and hoping for a crossing of the river at Blanchetaque (Point 2). His plans were, however, thwarted by other elements of the French army in the vicinity

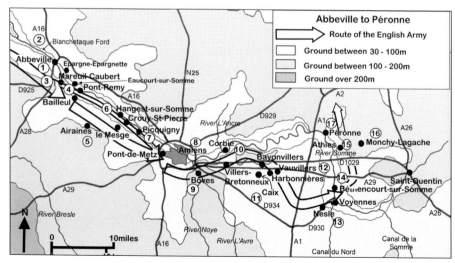

of Abbeville (Point 1) under the command of the constable, Charles d'Albret, the Duke of Alençon, Marshal Boucicaut, the Counts of Marle and Vendôme, the Sire de Rambures and Guichard Dauphin, grand master of the king's household. It is possible that other notable men with the army near Abbeville included the Count of Richemont, the Admiral of France, Clignet de Brabant, the Sire de Dampierre and the Bastard of Bourbon. The constable also drew on urban militias from Abbeville, Montreuil and Amiens to defend Blanchetaque and stake the ford to disrupt movement. Among the men from Amiens, sent somewhat reluctantly by the inhabitants, who feared for their own defence, were crossbowmen and *pavisiers* (shield-bearers for the crossbowmen). Artillery had also been sent to Abbeville.

We do not know for certain the French intentions at this stage. It may have been that they wanted to put on a show of strength near Blanchetaque to discourage Henry from crossing the Somme, since they would have known that this would force him inland along the bank of the river and thus buy them some time to continue to gather their army. Alternatively, it may have been that the French intention was not to prevent a crossing but rather to slow down the English and inflict casualties to weaken Henry's army and leave it in disarray as it emerged onto the north bank and found itself facing the bulk of the French army.

A surviving French battle plan, which may relate either to the period when the French were anticipating that Henry would attempt to cross the Somme at Blanchetaque or subsequently when he was near Péronne (Point 17) a few days later, envisaged the French army being divided into two main battles or divisions. The first of these, the vanguard, would comprise the men of Constable d'Albret on the right and Marshal Boucicaut on the left. The second battle was intended to consist of the companies of the Duke of Alençon and the Count of Eu. The army would also have two wings of men on foot, one on the right under the command of the Count of Richemont and the other on the left under the Count of Vendôme and Guichard Dauphin. Archers were to be positioned in front of each wing. The Sire de Rambures would command a company of heavy horse of up to 1,000 men, who would have the task of riding down the English archers. A further company of 200 mounted men-at-arms under Louis de Bosredon would be tasked with attacking the English baggage train and the rear of the English. If Henry's army fought in one division then the French planned to combine both their battles. The French clearly intended to maximize the effectiveness of their forces, which probably at this stage were not at full strength but may have amounted to around 6,000 men.

The March from Blanchetaque to the Crossing of the Somme

It is unlikely that Henry approached close to Blanchetaque with the main bulk of the English army. Intelligence from prisoners that there were some 6,000 men across the ford waiting for him, and confirmation from scouts that the ford was defended, even if they could not confirm numbers, was enough for Henry, and he turned towards the south-east parallel to the river Somme. His precise route south of Abbeville is uncertain. It is likely that Henry did not descend into the valley of the Somme with the greater part of the army but kept to the higher ground. However, he was still looking for somewhere to cross the river, and it is probable that he split his army, with part following the river valley.

By 13 October, when Henry was in the vicinity of Blanchetaque, it was becoming clear that his supplies would not be sufficient to get the army to Calais via the extended route that would now be required, even with the tactic of persuading town populations to exchange food for their safety. It now seems that foraging became more prevalent, with

Looking east to the valley of the Somme from Monts de Caubert, south of Abbeville, where the bulk of the English army marched while elements searched for crossing points in the valley below. (Peter Hoskins)

the army ranging far and wide. The lack of supplies as the march advanced, and indeed the suffering of the people, was exacerbated by a scorched earth policy adopted by the French as they passed through the area on their way beyond the Somme.

Marching on the higher ground parallel to the Somme would keep Henry safely away from any risk of harassment from the French army in the vicinity of Abbeville, and would also give him easier going on the firmer terrain of the plain above the river than the marshy ground in the Somme valley. Initially the two parts of the army were not too far apart, but at some point they probably diverged, with Henry taking the main body through Airaines (Point 5), which is consistent with reports of the army lodging at Bailleul. Airaines was no stranger to the passage of English armies, with Edward III having passed this way in 1346 before the Battle of Crécy, and it was fortified, unusually with two castles within the walls. The first of these, built in the twelfth century, was variously known as the chateau de l'Abbaye, because of its proximity to the priory and the church, and the chateau des Comtes de Ponthieu; the second, the chateau des Sires d'Airaines, was built in the thirteenth century. As with so many villages and towns in the area, the sire, John de Croy, died at Agincourt along with his son Archambault. Henry then turned east to skirt south of Amiens and crossed the river Avre near Boves (Point 9) before turning north-east to return to the Somme.

Meanwhile, on 14 October the part of the army in the valley looking for a crossing of the Somme approached a town, probably Pont-Rémy 8km upstream from Abbeville, but found the causeways broken and the French once again on the opposite bank. Pont-Rémy was protected by a castle to the south of the river, which itself gained some protection from a second arm of the river creating an island on which the castle stood. Henry appears to have anticipated some kind of engagement at Pont-Rémy since he created a number of knights. Indeed, there were claims of contact between the two armies with the Sire de Wancourt driving off the English. However, other sources simply state that the troops of the two armies faced each other, unable to approach sufficiently closely for combat due to the marshy ground. Whether Henry and the main body of the army came close to Pont-Rémy is not clear. Elements of the part of the army following the Somme are reported to have lodged at Mareuil, now part of Mareuil-Caubert (Point 3), near Pont-Rémy.

The broad, flat valley of the Somme near Pont Rémy and the ridge beyond where Henry marched with the main body of the army. (Peter Hoskins)

There was a series of castles along this stretch of the Somme, implying that there were several fords over the river to be monitored and controlled, including at Épagne-Épagnette, Eaucourt-sur-Somme (Point 4), Mareuil-Caubert and Pont-Rémy, which had resisted the crossing of Edward III's troops on their way along the Somme towards Blanchetaque in 1346. Pont-Rémy was in the County of Ponthieu, which had been held by English kings since 1279. The county had been confirmed as an English possession in 1360 under the terms of the Treaty of Brétigny, but Pont-Rémy was firmly back in French hands in 1415. It was taken and burnt by the Burgundians in 1421 and suffered further damage at their hands in 1433.

Beyond Airaines the bulk of the English army moved towards Boves, probably passing through the village of Le Mesge and then Pont-de-Metz, where, according to local tradition, Henry's men pillaged the town and vineyards, as it skirted to the south of Amiens (Point 8). The route remains across wide, open plains with Amiens visible from a considerable distance on a clear day. Meanwhile, the part of the army looking for crossing places and keeping closer to the river would have had to contend with marshy ground as the men skirted the small towns and villages built on ground slightly above the valley floor. They passed

Hangest-sur-Somme (Point 6), Crouy-St-Pierre and Picquigny (Point 7) until their route converged with that of the rest of the army near either Pont-de-Metz or Boves. Picquigny was surrounded by walls and towers and stood on cliffs above the Somme. It had four gates and since 1066 had had a stone castle, which had been rebuilt in the fourteenth century and was contiguous with the town walls. Repairs had been carried out in 1346 and again after the Battle of Poitiers. The Sire de Picquigny, Baudouin, died at Agincourt alongside two of his brothers-in-law.

After the failure to cross at Blanchetaque, Henry's chances of finding a crossing upstream towards Amiens were thin. The river course was more or less in a straight line so it was easy for the French to keep pace with the English. In addition, there was high ground on the north bank of the river rising steeply almost 100m above the river valley for much of the way between Abbeville and Amiens. The marshy terrain in the river valley, combined with this topography, would have made a safe crossing of the Somme and a subsequent exit from the river valley difficult in the best of circumstances. With French forces to contend with, it would have been very hazardous.

Henry probably passed to the south of Amiens on 15 October, and may have arrayed his army in anticipation of a French attack; in the event this did not materialize. Beyond Amiens the land changes a little in character on the approach to Boves. It can hardly be called hilly, but the variations in elevation become more pronounced and the castle of Boves stands out on the skyline from some distance. Even though today it is a ruin and is surrounded by trees, its position some 55m above the valley of the Avre is impressive. On a clear day Amiens is visible from the castle, and the progress of the English army was probably followed for some time before its arrival. Both the town and the castle at Boves belonged to the Count of Vaudémont. He was a supporter of the Duke of Burgundy, and, although he was away serving with the French, the reaction in Boves to the passage of the English was something of a test of Burgundy's loyalty. The garrison behaved much as other towns had done, exchanging food for the safety of the town and surrounding countryside. Eight baskets of bread were supplied. Since two men were required to carry each basket, the weight of bread would have been substantial, but the rations would not have gone far with an army the size of Henry's. The captain of the castle, Sir John de Matringueham,

Boves castle seen on the line of approach of Henry V. Amiens is clearly visible from the site of the castle and the garrison would probably have had early warning of the approach of the English. (Peter Hoskins)

View from Boves Castle across the village and the river Avre to the east. (Richard Kinnear)

took in two very sick men from Henry's army, with a ransom of two horses each being provided in surety for their release when they had returned to health.

The most straightforward descent into the valley of the Avre is to the north-west of Boves, just to the north of the D116. There is an easy exit from the valley beyond the town for the route of the onward march which crosses a ridge and then descends to the Somme once again and Corbie (Point 10), which lies on the far bank of the river.

Corbie was well fortified with walls and eighteen towers that had been constructed in 1343. It was garrisoned under the captaincy of Pierre de Lameth and Gauthier de Caulincourt. There was an engagement here between the French and the English. It may be that the garrison made a sortie, but it is possible that this contact between the French and the English took place a little to the south of Corbie, on the higher ground near Villers-Bretonneux. In any case, Henry's men had the better of the encounter, driving off the French and taking at least two prisoners. From these prisoners the French plan to use squadrons of cavalry to ride down the English archers was discovered, which led to a rumour running through the English army. It may be that it was at this stage of the campaign, and in view of this information, that Henry gave orders for each archer to prepare a stake, 1.8m long and sharpened at both ends, to drive into the ground for protection against cavalry. After this engagement a soldier was brought before Henry, charged with having stolen a pyx from a local church. He was hanged for the offence.

There is no suggestion that Henry expected to cross the Somme at Corbie, but he needed to do so soon if he were not to be driven further and further away from his objective of Calais. After Corbie he made directly towards Nesle (Point 13), either passing through or billeting the army in the villages of Bayonvillers, Harbonnières (where there was a castle taken by the English twenty-five years later), Caix (Point 11) and Vauvillers (Point 12). At least one of the inhabitants of Caix had answered the call to arms. The squire Galois de Chey was recorded as serving in the company of Raoul de Gaucourt, and was probably present at the siege of Harfleur.

From Nesle Henry could turn north-east to cross the Somme south of Péronne, and as he moved towards the town Henry had the advantage of moving across the chord of a wide bend in the river. The

Harbonnières from the south, one of four villages in close proximity to one another where Henry's army may have lodged on the approach to Nesle, showing the wide, open plains in this area. (Peter Hoskins)

French forces moving along the far bank would have to follow this bend. The difference in distance was not great, perhaps 16km or so between Corbie and the eventual crossing point in the vicinity of Béthencourt-sur-Somme (Point 14) and Voyennes, but it was enough to enable Henry to draw ahead by about half a day's march, and with this advantage he now had a better chance of getting across the river than he had had hitherto. From Corbie to Nesle the going would have been easy, with only the slightest undulations in the wide open plain above the valley of the Somme. Today wind turbines, water towers and industrial buildings intrude into the landscape, but even so the churches stand out on the skyline, giving a good impression of the scattered nature of the habitation of this area of relatively low population density. It is the kind of country where movement could be detected far off, and the chances of the French ambushing or surprising Henry's men would have been slight.

The French had moved through Corbie and were in Péronne around 19 October, the date that Henry crossed the river about 19km to the south. The land to the south of Péronne would have suited the French well for battle, and it may be that they were content to see the English cross the river at last. Nevertheless, finding the crossing must have come as a great relief for Henry's men, since there is some evidence that they thought that they might have to go as far to the east as St-Quentin; crossing south of Péronne, therefore, saved them perhaps eight days' marching.

On 18 October Henry had attempted to negotiate a trade of food for safety with the inhabitants of Nesle. The inhabitants refused the offer, possibly because they felt safe behind their defences. There was a substantial castle within the walls, with eight towers and walls 18m high, and the town itself was surrounded by ramparts. The river Ingon, which was navigable in the Middle Ages, ran on the south-west side and on the other sides were wide, deep ditches fed by the river. In addition, there were five outlying forts in an arc a few hundred metres from the town facing the direction of approach of Henry and his army. As a consequence of the refusal of the inhabitants to agree to his offer,

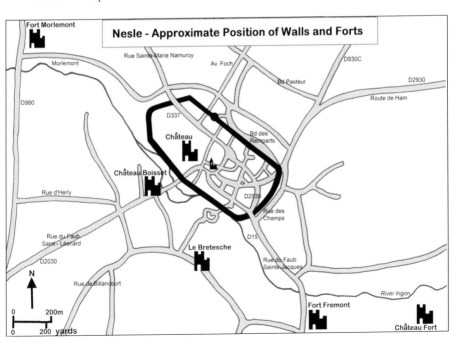

Henry ordered that the area should be torched the following day. It seems that the orders were not carried out, perhaps because news of a crossing point had arrived.

Several places were recorded by the chroniclers as the site of the English crossing of the Somme: Éclusier-Vaux to the north-west of Péronne, somewhere between Péronne and St-Quentin, Doingt, slightly to the east of Péronne, and between Béthencourt-sur-Somme and Voyennes. This latter place is the most probable crossing point.

It is possible that the inhabitants of Nesle, although feeling secure within the walls of the town, may not have been so sanguine about property outside the walls and so gave the location of the crossing point to the English to divert them from plunder and destruction. According to local tradition, the ford across the marshland and the river was betrayed to the English by a local inhabitant, although this may be no more than a story seeking to explain away the failure of the French to prevent the crossing. The truth may be much more straightforward, since fords across the river were probably well known, with a castle existing at Béthencourt (demolished in the seventeenth century on King Louis XIII's orders) to guard the ford.

Orders had been given on the French side to prevent the use of crossings, and it has been suggested that the crossing used by Henry should have been staked but that those responsible had failed to do so. Presumably the garrison of the castle at Béthencourt, if it had one, was too small to have any impact on the crossing.

Once the crossing place had been identified, the army had to advance across marshy terrain between the Somme and another unidentified river, possibly the Ingon, which runs through Nesle. Once they reached the Somme, the crossing is reported as consisting of two narrow causeways that had not been staked but had been broken in the middle of the river. However, a crossing could still be made in single file. Men-at-arms and archers under the command of Sir John Cornwall and Sir Gilbert Umfraville, both of whom had been involved in the initial reconnaissance when Henry had landed, were therefore sent across to establish a bridgehead to protect the crossing of the bulk of the army. Henry gave orders for the causeways to be repaired, using faggots, straw and planks. Some accounts talk of the English demolishing houses and taking shutters, windows and ladders to bridge the gaps. Others describe the English commandeering labourers and carpenters to fell trees and construct a bridge. The crossing seems to have been carried out with remarkable discipline. Archers crossed first to create a defensive bridgehead, a standard was planted, and then the remainder of the vanguard crossed, followed by the centre division and the rear-guard. Realising the importance of avoiding congestion, Henry and his senior lieutenants took a hands-on approach to managing the crossing, positioning themselves by the two causeways to marshal the crossing of men, horses and vehicles, with one causeway used for wagons and the other for troops. Reports of the time taken for the crossing vary, but it must have taken several hours and it seems that it was close to nightfall, around 5.00 p.m., before all of the army was safely across.

The day after the crossing the army advanced little more than 8km, across ground initially more undulating than on the approach to the river, lodging for the night of 20 October in the vicinity of the villages of Athies (Point 15) and Monchy-Lagache (Point 16). Athies was fortified with a wall, built of brick, in an oval pattern. There was also a castle to the north-east of the village, defended with a double curtain wall, which fell into disuse and was demolished in the eighteenth century. Unlike many local lords, Gérard d'Athies survived the Battle of Agincourt and in 1421 fought for the Burgundians, then allied to the English, against the dauphin at the Battle of Mons-en-Vimeux.

The Route by Car
This tour starts in Abbeville (Point 1) and rejoins the route of Henry V's army after visiting his intended crossing point of the Somme at Blanchetaque (Point 2, also covered in Tour 2). To visit Blanchetaque, leave Abbeville on the D40 to Port-le-Grand. In the village, turn left by the railway halt, cross the railway and turn right to continue on the Chemin de Valois. Take the third turning to the left after about 2km. The turning is signposted Station Biologique de Blanchetaque et Ferme des Bouchers. From Blanchetaque, retrace the route along the Chemin des Valois to Port-le-Grand, follow the D40 towards Abbeville for about 800m, then turn right onto the D86. Turn left onto the D3 and follow this road to the D925 at Cambron. Follow the D925 towards Abbeville. About 800m after passing under the A28 motorway the road turns left through a right-angle. Immediately after this bend, turn right and follow the D3 through Mareuil-Caubert (Point 3) to Bray-lès-Mareuil. Turn left onto an unnumbered road to Épagne-Épagnette, and then right onto

the D901 to Eaucourt-sur-Somme (Point 4). Continue on the D901 to Airaines (Point 5). From Airaines follow the D936 to Soues and turn left onto the D69 to Hangest-sur-Somme (Point 6). Follow the D3 to Picquigny (Point 7) and then the D1235 to Amiens (Point 8).

Take the D116 from Amiens to Boves (Point 9). From Boves take the D167 to Corbie (Point 10). From Corbie follow the D122 to Lamotte-Warfusée. Continue on the D1029, and after about 1.5km turn right onto the D337 to Bayonvillers. Take the D165 to Caix (Point 11) and then follow the D28 to Rosières-en-Santerre and then the D229 to Vauvillers (Point 12). Retrace your steps on the D229 to the D337 and turn left to follow this road to Nesle (Point 13).

From Nesle take the D15 to Béthencourt-sur-Somme (Point 14). The likely crossing place of the Somme was probably somewhere between this village and Voyennes. Cross the bridge over the canal on the D15. A good view of the river can be had just after crossing the canal. Stay on the D15 through Croix Moligneaux to Monchy-Lagache (Point 16). Leave on the same road initially and then follow the D45 and D937 to Athies (Point 15). From Athies follow the D937 through Doingt to Péronne (Point 17).

The Route on Foot and by Bike

The walking and cycling route for this tour follows that taken by the part of the army looking for a crossing place of the Somme and then rejoins the route of the main army near Amiens. The distance is 175km. Much of the route is on minor roads, but with some use of long-distance footpaths. A variation on the route takes in the ford of Blanchetaque (Point 2). This increases the walking distance by 22km. Most of this additional walking is along a canal towpath.

The Blanchetaque Variant

Leave Abbeville (Point 1) on the towpath on the southern bank of the Canal Maritime d'Abbeville à St-Valery and continue to the D86. Turn right to follow this road through Petit-Port to the D40. Turn left and follow the road into Port-le-Grand. In the village turn left to cross the railway line on the crossing, and turn right to follow the unnumbered road for 2km. The road turns left to the Chalet du Gué de Blanche Taque. (Note: do not be tempted to stay on the towpath beyond the D86: the track on the map between the canal and the chalet past the Ferme des

Bouchers is private and not open to the public.) From Blanchetaque, retrace your steps to the canal towpath. On approaching Abbeville, leave the canal at the first bridge after passing under the motorway. Follow an unnumbered road and turn right onto the D925 through Rouvroy. Just after the junction with the D3, as the D925 turns sharply right, turn left to follow the Ancien Chemin de Blangy to climb onto the ridge above the Somme on the Monts de Caubert. Stay on this track until you reach a T-junction after just over 3km. Turn left and, on an unnumbered road, cross the D928 and continue to the D3. Turn right towards Mareuil-Caubert (Point 3) to rejoin the main route from Abbeville.

> *The Ancien Chemin de Blangy, on the Blanchetaque Variant route, is partly paved, but much of the surface is made of compacted earth and stones. An alternative route for cyclists is along the D3 from Rouvroy to join the main route at the junction with the D928.*

Main Route

Leave Abbeville on an unnumbered road just to the west of the Somme until it joins the D928. Follow the road to the intersection with the D3 and turn left to follow this road through Mareuil-Caubert. About 1.5km beyond Bray-lès-Mareuil turn left onto an unnumbered road through Erondelle. To visit Pont-Rémy, turn left on the D901. To continue without visiting Pont-Rémy, continue on the unnumbered road until it rejoins the D3. Follow this road once again to Longpré-les-Corps-Saints. Turn left and follow the D216 until it swings sharply left in Condé-Folie. Turn right along the D218, which is a quieter option than the D3. Continue on this road to Hangest-sur-Somme (Point 6) and then rejoin the D3 to Picquigny (Point 7). As you leave the town turn right onto the Rue de la Vigne and take the first left to join the *GR123*. This path is not well way-marked but is easy to follow with a 1:25,000 scale map. As the *GR123* swings south-west just before the village of Dreuil-lès-Amiens there are two options for the onward journey to Amiens (Point 8). The first option is to turn left almost immediately onto a track which intersects an unnumbered road that can be followed through Dreuil-lès-Amiens and then alongside a railway line until it joins the D211 on the outskirts of Amiens. The alternative route is to continue on the *GR123* until the path swings right and heads west. Continue straight on to Saveuse and then take the D211 into Amiens.

> Just after Picquigny stretches of the GR123 used on the main walking route have a surface of stones and compacted earth. An alternative route for cyclists is to follow the D1235 (formerly the N235) into Amiens.

From Amiens follow the D116 to Boves (Point 9) and then the D167 to Corbie (Point 10). To visit the castle ruins in Boves, turn right onto a steep track, the Chemin des Ruines, on entering the village just as the Rue Gaston Lecomte swings left. Follow this track until the intersection with the D167. Take this road past the cemetery and then the next left onto an unpaved track. The ruins are not signposted, but can be found by taking a path up through the woods. Return to Boves on the D167 and rejoin the route to Corbie.

> The Chemin des Ruines in Boves is initially paved but the last stretch is along a packed earth and stone surface. An alternative route to the ruins for the cyclist is to continue on the D116 to the intersection with the D167 and turn right to follow this road, and then rejoin the walking route.

Leave Corbie on the D1 towards Fouilloy. Turn left onto the D71 just before the village, and after about 400m turn right onto the D122. Follow this road to the junction with the D1029 in Lamotte-Warfusée. Cross the D1029 and follow an unnumbered road to Bayonvillers. Follow the D337 from Bayonvillers to Harbonnières. From Harbonnières take an unnumbered road running to the east of, and roughly parallel to, the D41 to Caix (Point 11).

> The unnumbered road towards Caix is paved until about 800m beyond the railway line. There is then a stretch of track of about 1.5km with a stone and packed earth surface which in places is badly rutted and potholed. Alternative routes for cyclists are either to take the D41 from Harbonnières to Caix or to cut out Caix and turn left for Rosières-en-Santerre on the unnumbered road immediately having crossed the railway line.

Leave Caix to the east on the D28 to Rosières-en-Santerre, and then follow the D39 through Méharicourt, Chilly and Punchy. Approximately 1.5km beyond Punchy cross the D1017 and take an unnumbered road to join the D337 into Curchy.

The track between the D1017 and the D337 is paved for some stretches, but the surface has deteriorated badly and the packed stone and earth surface on other stretches is badly rutted and potholed in places. It can be muddy in wet weather. An alternative route for cyclists is to turn left onto the D1017 from the D39 and then right onto the D337 to Curchy.

Leave Curchy on an unnumbered road, initially running south of and parallel to the D337. In Manicourt turn right for about 250m, and then turn left onto a track running parallel to, and about 600m south of, the D337. Follow the track across the D930 past Morlemont farm and turn right onto the Rue Ste-Marie Namuroy into the centre of Nesle (Point 13).

The track from Manicourt is made of packed earth and stone. It is deeply rutted and potholed, and is muddy in wet weather. Beyond the crossing of the D930 the track is paved for a short distance but quickly changes to an earth surface. It seems to be used rarely and the grass can be thigh high. An alternative route for cyclists is to take the D249 and D337 from Manicourt to Nesle.

Leave Nesle on the D930c to the Canal du Nord. Turn left to follow the towpath alongside the canal to Béthencourt-sur-Somme (Point 14). Cross the canal on the D15, and from Villecourt follow unnumbered roads to Falvy. Turn right and follow the D103 to Athies (Point 15). Leave the village to the north following an unnumbered road, which initially runs just to the west of the D937, to Brie.

Part of the road from Athies to Brie is paved, but there are stretches with a surface of packed earth and stone. It is badly rutted in places and can be muddy in wet weather. An alternative for cyclists is to take the D937 from Athies and then turn left just after la Plaine Ferme to rejoin the route in Mesnil-Bruntel.

Turn right onto the D88 and just before Mesnil-Bruntel turn left onto an unnumbered road, identifiable with its no-entry sign for vehicles, annotated *sauf riverains*, for about 300m. Turn right onto the Chemin de Bas and after about 200m turn left into the Rue du Jeu de Paume past Ferme de Brunte to Flamicourt on the outskirts of Péronne (Point 17). In Flamicourt turn right and follow the Rue Roger Corne to join the D199 into Péronne.

What to See
Abbeville
Point 1: See Tour 2, Point 16, page 87.

Blanchetaque
Point 2: See Tour 2, Point 15, page 86.

Mareuil-Caubert
Point 3: Part of the English army passed this way looking for a crossing over the Somme. The church of St Christophe on the D3 (GPS 50.068465, 1.830001) was built in the eleventh century. It was partially destroyed in 1346, probably by Edward III's army as it moved down the Somme towards Blanchetaque. The façade, nave and some of the choir survived, and repairs and additions were made during the fourteenth

The church of St Christophe in Mareuil-Caubert. (Peter Hoskins)

and fifteenth centuries. The wooden porch in front of the north door dates from the sixteenth century. There was also a castle at Mareuil-Caubert on the higher ground about 150m north-west of the church.

Eaucourt-sur-Somme
Point 4: The castle at Eaucourt-sur-Somme, in the Rue du Pont close to the Somme, was one of a number of castles along the stretch of river between Abbeville and Amiens where Henry's scouts searched for crossings. Along with other similar castles along the river, it suffered at the hands of the Burgundians in 1421 (GPS 50.062077, 1.881364). However, some vestiges remain and a number of activities are organized here during the summer: www.chateau-eaucourt.com.

The remains of the castle at Eaucourt-sur-Somme. (Peter Hoskins)

Airaines
Point 5: Henry V took the main part of his army through Airaines while his scouts were looking for a crossing of the Somme in the valley below. The priory church of Notre-Dame in the Rue des Buttes (GPS 49.9625,

The church of Notre-Dame in Airaines.
(Peter Hoskins)

1.939444) was built around 1130. The adjoining priory was destroyed during the Burgundian occupation in 1422 and rebuilt in the sixteenth century. The original parish church of St Denis in the Rue St Denis (GPS 49.965094, 1.945351) was also built in the twelfth century, but the current building dates from the sixteenth century. The chateau de l'Abbaye, or the chateau des Comtes de Ponthieu, stood on the hill approximately 150m to the north-west of the church of Notre-Dame. The castle had been garrisoned by the Burgundians in 1422. It was razed by King Louis XI in 1472, and only the motte remains, which can be

Les Tours de Luynes on the site of the château des Sires d'Airaines.
(Peter Hoskins)

seen from the Rue du Chateau de Ponthieu (GPS 49.963051, 1.93856). The chateau des Sires d'Airaines was destroyed in the sixteenth century and a new castle was built on the same site the following century. Two towers of the later castle, known as Les Tours de Luynes, survive in the Rue de Luynes (GPS 49.965135,1.939826).

Hangest-sur-Somme
Point 6: Scouts looking for a crossing of the Somme passed via Hangest. The church of Ste Marguerite, Rue Jean Baptiste Carpentier, with its thirteenth-century bell tower, survives (GPS 49.979855, 2.06518).

The church of Ste Marguerite in Hangest-sur-Somme. (Peter Hoskins)

Picquigny
Point 7: Picquigny was a well defended town that lay on the route of the part of the army following the valley of the Somme. At St-Pierre-à-Gouy, about 1.5km north-west of Picquigny on the D3, is the ruined Abbaye du Gard (GPS 49.960913, 2.108925), founded in the twelfth century. The abbey is not open to the public. There are substantial remains of the castle in the town (GPS 49.942904, 2.142302). The interiors of the buildings are not open to visitors, but the grounds and

Construction of the church of St Martin in Picquigny started in 1066. (Peter Hoskins)

The fourteenth-century barbican of Picquigny Castle. (Peter Hoskins)

exterior are, nevertheless, worth seeing. The twelfth- and thirteenth-century collegiate church of St Martin (GPS 49.943166, 2.142173), built to replace an earlier castle chapel, is within the curtilage of the castle.

Amiens
Point 8: The citizens of Amiens, concerned over the possible impact on their own safety by the despatch of arms and men to join the French army, would no doubt have been relieved to see the English pass to their south. The town has a rich heritage of buildings from across the centuries. The highlight is the thirteenth-century cathedral of Notre-Dame in the Place Notre Dame (GPS 49.894849, 2.300595). In the Place au Fil is the fourteenth-century belfry (GPS 49.895488, 2.295986), built between 1406 and 1410. It originally included a watch tower. The current bell tower above the fifteenth-century base was added in the eighteenth century.

Amiens Cathedral.
(Peter Hoskins)

Boves

Point 9: The garrison of Boves, like those of so many towns in Henry's path, traded the safety of the town in return for supplies of food for the English army. There are some vestiges of the castle just to the east of the D167 to the south of the town (GPS 49.843424, 2.379372). The castle keep was built on a man-made motte on a ridge above the town and it was surrounded by a ditch and earth ramparts. It originally included two baileys. The upper bailey enclosed the priory, now the Ferme du Prieuré, and the lower surrounded the town. There is a curious claim in a local history that it was sacked in 1443 by the Duke of Bedford, who had died eight years earlier. It was finally destroyed at the end of the sixteenth century. Heading south on the D167 from Boves, turn left onto a track shortly after passing the cemetery on your left. It is possible to park a car here, but access to the ruins requires a steep climb up a path through the woods.

The remains of the castle keep at Boves.
(Richard Kinnear)

Corbie

Point 10: Henry passed Corbie on his way to his eventual crossing of the Somme. There was a minor engagement with the French somewhere in the vicinity. The twelfth-century church of St Etienne, now deconsecrated, survives in the Place John Catelas (GPS 49.909616, 2.508745). There are the remains of a watch tower, or *échauguette*, once on the town walls, in the grounds of the Lycée Professionel Privé Ste Colette along the Rue de l'Enclos (GPS 49.91028, 2.51028).

Corbie, the church of St Etienne.
(Peter Hoskins)

Remains of an échauguette or watch tower on the town wall in Corbie. (Richard Kinnear)

The church of Ste Croix in Caix. (Peter Hoskins)

Caix

Point 11: Henry V is reported to have lodged in Caix, with the army dispersed between the village and three other settlements nearby: Bayonvillers, Harbonnières and Vauvillers. The choir and the transept of the church of Ste Croix in the Rue de l'Église (GPS 49.8158, 2.645547) date from the second half of the thirteenth century. The castle in the village was burnt down and the nave of the church damaged in the early fifteenth century in fighting between the Burgundians and the Armagnacs.

Vauvillers

Point 12: The tower and the transept of the church of St Éloi in the Rue de Caix (GPS 49.848451, 2.703225) in Vauvillers, where some of the English army lodged while Henry was nearby at Caix, date from the twelfth century.

The church of St Eloi in Vauvillers. (Peter Hoskins)

Nesle

Point 13: It was when the English army was in the vicinity of Nesle that Henry V finally found a crossing of the Somme. The town's medieval castle and forts no longer exist. The sites of two of the forts are recalled in place names: Morlement (GPS 49.762479, 2.895150) to the north-west of the town and le Chateau Fort (GPS 49.751064, 2.918673) to the east. The Chateau Boisset, previously a Templar fortress, stood close to the Rue du Faubourg St-Léonard (GPS 49.756165, 2.903373). Nesle's collegiate church of Notre-Dame is a twentieth-century church built in 1930 to replace the earlier eleventh-century building, the original church having been destroyed in 1918 when a delayed action fuse, set by withdrawing German troops as allied forces approached, detonated explosives stored in the crypt. Both the church and the eighteenth-

Vestiges of the castle in Nesle, destroyed in 1918. (Peter Hoskins)

century chateau opposite were destroyed. A fragment of the castle perimeter wall remains in the Place de la République (49.757243, 2.907235), but its date is not certain.

Béthencourt-sur-Somme
Point 14: Henry's army probably crossed the Somme between Béthencourt and Voyennes. The nature of the Somme has changed much since the fifteenth century with the construction of canals, and it is difficult to visualize how it would have looked as Henry's army approached in 1415. It can also be difficult to get a clear view of the river, with much of it now shielded from view by trees and houses. However, just to the east of Béthencourt (GPS 49.795256, 2.966992), beyond the canal bridge, a clear view of the river shows how the low-lying ground results in an extensive patchwork of pools and lakes interlocking with the river proper. Before the construction of the canals much of the low-

The Somme at Béthencourt-sur-Somme. (Peter Hoskins)

lying land adjacent to the river would have been marsh susceptible to flooding.

Athies
Point 15: The English lodged in the vicinity of Athies and Monchy-Lagache after crossing the Somme. The site of the ramparts to the south of the village can still be traced along the line of the Chemin Sous la Ville with a section of buttressed brick-built wall towards the eastern end (GPS 49.85267, 2.983022). There are said to be further remains of the fortifications of the village, including another length of wall to the north and a section of ditch near the residential retirement home, la Maison de Retraite, in the Rue de Ste Radegonde (GPS 49.855496, 2.983259).

The church of Notre Dame de l'Assomption (GPS 49.854775, 2.979344) was seriously damaged in the First World War, but thirteenth-century sculptures survive on the south door.

A stretch of the town ramparts in the Chemin-sous-la Ville in Athies. (Peter Hoskins)

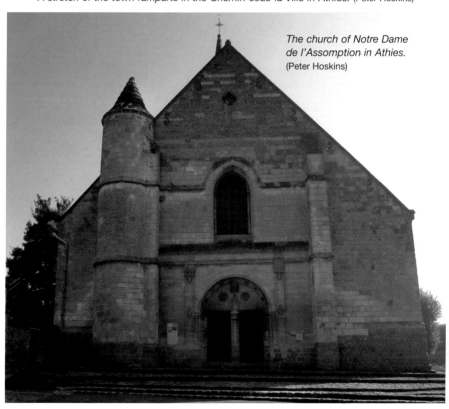

The church of Notre Dame de l'Assomption in Athies. (Peter Hoskins)

Monchy-Lagache

Point 16: Henry's men lodged near here and Athies after crossing the Somme. The parish church of St Pierre, in the Grande Rue (GPS 49.853563, 3.04479), has elements from the twelfth and fifteenth centuries, but the clock tower, dynamited by German troops in 1917, was rebuilt in 1922.

Péronne

Point 17: The French commanders met in Péronne on 19 October 1415 while the English were crossing the Somme between Voyennes and Béthencourt-sur-Somme. The castle, in Place André Audinot (GPS 49.929096, 2.932255), was badly damaged

The church of St Pierre in Monchy-Lagache. (Richard Kinnear)

during the First World War, but it has been restored and now houses the First World War museum: Historial de la Grande Guerre.

The thirteenth-century castle in Péronne. (Peter Hoskins)

Maps

Maps at 1:25,000, 1:50,000 and 1:100,000 Scales
Published by the *Institut National de l'Information Géographique et Forestière (IGN)* www.ign.fr

Cartes de Randonnée – 1:25,000		
2207O – Abbeville	2308O – Amiens	2409O – Harbonnières
2107OT – Tréport	2309E – Moreuil	2409E – Roye
2208O – Hallencourt	2308E – Corbie	2509O – Nesle
2208E – Picquigny	2408O – Albert	2508O – Péronne
Série Orange – 1:50,000		
M2207 – Abbeville	M2308 – Amiens	M2509 – Ham
M2208 – Hallencourt	M2408 – Albert	M2508 – Péronne
M2309 – Moreuil	M2409 – Roye	The *IGN* catalogue does not list a 1:50,000 map covering the 1:25,000 map 2107OT.

TOP 100 – 1:100,000
TOP100103 – Amiens/Arras

How to Get There and Back by Public Transport

Beauvais, Lille and Paris airports are all practical for this tour. There is a shuttle bus service from Beauvais to the centre of Paris and there are good transport links from the Paris airports to the city centre. Lille airport has a shuttle bus service to the railway stations in the city. Abbeville can be reached by rail from Paris and Lille. Péronne is within the Picardie *TER* region, but the final part of the service is provided by buses on which bicycles cannot be carried. For cyclists alternative access to and from Péronne is by *TGV* to the station TGV Haute-Picardie 14km south-west of Péronne near Éstrées-Deniécourt. A number of intermediate towns on the route have railway stations, with Picquigny, Hangest-sur-Somme, Corbie and Nesle operated by Picardie region *TER*. Some services are provided by buses on which bicycles cannot be carried.

Where to Stay and Where to Eat
The websites listed below give information on local accommodation and restaurants for this tour:

www.abbeville-tourisme.com
www.visit-somme.com (in English) and www.somme-tourisme.com
www.amiens-tourisme.com
www.tourisme-corbie-bocage-3-vallées.com
www.picardietourisme.com

Abbeville, Amiens, Corbie, Harbonnières, Rosières-en-Santerre, Nesle and Péronne have places where refreshments can be found. There are also some bars and restaurants in a number of villages along the route.

Tour Four
Péronne to Calais via Agincourt

From the Crossing of the Somme to Calais, via the Battlefield
This tour starts at Péronne and follows the route of Henry's advance after his crossing of the Somme just to the south of the town on 19 October to his arrival at Maisoncelle on the eve of battle five days later, 24 October, and then to Calais via the battlefield at Agincourt. It covers 204km.

What Happened
Henry V's Crossing of the Somme and the Assembly of the French
By around nightfall on 19 October 1415 Henry's army was safely across the river Somme near Béthencourt-sur-Somme (Point 2). The French were taken by surprise by the crossing. Some patrols probed the bridgehead to see if they could push the English back, but they were too late. English mounted patrols drove them off, and the period of vulnerability passed as Henry's strength on the far bank increased. The problem for the French had been that potential crossing points became more numerous the further the English moved upstream, and with a long stretch of area to watch they had had to disperse their troops in small groups. The slow communications of the period and the time required to then reassemble the army meant that they could not marshal sufficient troops in time to oppose Henry's crossing.

On the day the English were crossing the river, the French held a council 19km away in Péronne (Point 1). Present were the Dukes of Bourbon and Alençon, the Counts of Richemont, Eu and Vendôme, Guichard Dauphin, Constable d'Albret, Marshal Boucicaut, the Seneschal of Hainault and the Lords of Waurin and Rons. Even if they were not yet aware of Henry's crossing when they met, they would have known that it must happen soon. Many senior members of the French

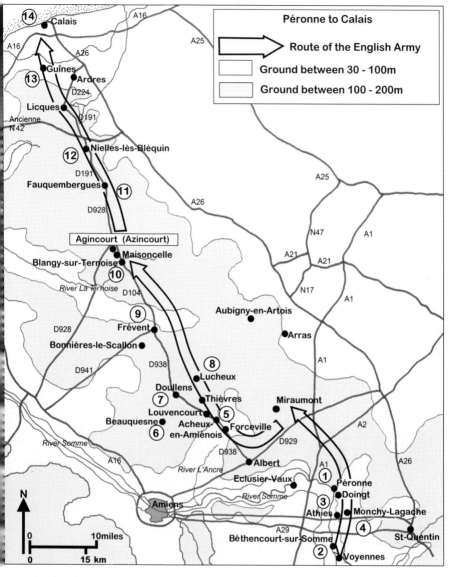

leadership were still at Rouen and the king's council met there, either on 20 October or perhaps earlier. A minority in the French camp advised caution, and there were some, including the Duke of Berry, whose father King John II had been captured at Poitiers in 1356, who warned that if the tide of fortune turned against them it would be better to lose a battle than a battle and a king. With the majority in favour of battle the decision was taken to fight, but in recognition of the warnings of those counselling caution it was decided that neither the king nor the dauphin would be present at the battle. With these decisions taken, the French knew that they had to act quickly to intercept Henry, who was now only about a week's march from the safety of Calais. They needed to draw in further lords and their troops from northern parts of the realm, and amongst these was the Duke of Brabant. He was in Louvain at the time, about 190km from Péronne. That he received a request from the council in Péronne to come in person only two days after the council met testifies to the urgency of the situation. Further decisive action taken by the French was the despatch of heralds on 20 October to inform Henry of the intent to bring him to battle before he reached Calais.

There are discrepancies between accounts of who was present at the two councils in Péronne and Rouen, and there is uncertainty over which council issued the despatch to Henry, and in whose name. It was possibly sent from Rouen but more probably from Péronne, although there may have been coordination between the two. With both the king and the dauphin intending to stay away from the battle, and the Duke of Berry being too old to fight, the Duke of Orléans, as the next senior member of the royal family, was the logical person to issue the call to Henry to join battle. He, however, was in Orléans on 17 October. If, as seems probable, Orléans and Burgundy had initially been ordered to stay away to avoid opening old wounds, then around this date Orléans was summoned to come north to join the gathering army.

The summons to Henry may have proposed a site for the battle at Aubigny-en-Artois, and the French may have believed that Henry had accepted this location. It is possible that the French set out for Aubigny from Péronne while Henry was still south of the town, and that they crossed his line of march as they moved north-east. In the event Henry did not go to Aubigny, and the French army had to redeploy towards Agincourt to intercept him when they discovered that Henry was not coming to meet them. This may explain in part why elements of the French army were absent from the battle. There are numerous accounts of the French summons and Henry's response, but it is likely that Henry's goal remained to get to Calais without giving battle should that prove to be possible.

By the time Henry reached Maisoncelle he had marched some 400km since leaving Harfleur. His men had been involved in some minor operations and the army had suffered a small number of casualties in minor engagements. Henry had deliberately avoided making assaults on large towns, and although he had lodged in Boves he generally avoided staying in walled towns. He had left behind at Harfleur his artillery and siege equipment, but nevertheless there would have been a considerable baggage train with carts and beasts of burden for victuals, supplies for the archers and personal baggage for the more important men in the army. He had averaged around 24km a day, which was a good pace of advance, in particular since the army had not rested on the march. Henry placed great importance on the discipline and correct conduct of his army. The men would certainly have foraged for food as they advanced, but in general the pillaging, burning and destruction that typically accompanied such activities seems to have been less than would have been expected from an English army in the time of Edward III in the previous century. Indeed, it seems that the villagers and townspeople suffered more from the passage of the French than they did from Henry's men.

The English March from the Somme to Maisoncelle
Having crossed the river, the army advanced a short distance and lodged near the villages of Athies (Point 3) and Monchy-Lagache (Point 4). Now across the Somme, the English, according to one chronicler travelling with the army, were in high spirits. There were no further significant obstacles between them and Calais, and they thought they had shaved several days off their journey. They also thought they had stolen a march on the French, who they believed were further to the east. The feeling also seemed to be abroad that the French would be disinclined to follow them. We do not know whether or not Henry shared these illusions, but within twenty-four hours of the crossing the French heralds had come to him with the challenge to join battle.

The next day, 21 October, Henry moved off to the north-west, with the terrain once more becoming open and with almost imperceptible undulations, and passed through Doingt, which had a castle to the west of the town. It is said locally that the castle was occupied by Henry's troops on the way to Agincourt, but in view of Henry's aim to reach Calais this seems unlikely. As he passed through Doingt the fortified town of Péronne was some 4km to his left. About 1.5km beyond Péronne his men found the roads had been churned up by the passage of many thousands of men and horses. This was probably the French army moving towards Aubigny on 21 October. According to some accounts Henry had already given orders for his archers to be equipped with stakes (see page 99), but it may have been at this stage that he gave these orders, given the likelihood of battle. Henry also put on his armour and ordered the army to do likewise. There seems to have been considerable consternation, verging on panic, within the English army at the prospect of imminent battle with what they may now have realized was a much larger French force. Henry was prudently taking action to be ready for battle.

Henry's army is reported to have now moved in the direction of Albert (known as Ancre until it was renamed by King Louis XIII in honour of its newly appointed lord, Charles d'Albert), a well defended town with walls, four fortified gates and a castle to the east integrated within the town walls. In response to the threat posed by a campaign by Edward III in 1359 the defences had been repaired and new ditches dug. In 1411 further measures had been taken to repair the fortifications. This had led to a dispute between the lord and the townspeople on one side and the prior on the other. The prior asserted that the Church had no obligation to contribute to the repairs, but under pressure agreed, without prejudice to his rights, to make a contribution. However, the dispute dragged on and it was only in March 1415 that it was resolved and a loan raised, repayable over three years, to finance the work. How far the repairs had progressed by October is not known.

However, despite the suggestion that he moved towards Albert, the first recorded town that the army passed by after leaving the vicinity of Péronne was Miraumont. Henry subsequently turned more to the west, but the army probably passed 10km north of Albert. If English troops came close to the town they were probably scouts or foragers rather than the main body of the army. In any case, Albert would have been safe from a major attack in view of Henry's approach throughout the march of not attacking fortified towns.

If the French did challenge Henry to join them in battle at Aubigny-en-Artois, about 18km west of Arras, then the route towards Miraumont suggests that Henry initially set off in that direction. The subsequent change of direction implies that the initial move was either a feint to convince the French that he had accepted their challenge, or that having initially set off towards Aubigny and the gathering French army he had changed his mind. The most probable explanation is that he was not seeking a fight, and that the move to Miraumont and then the change of direction were intended to deceive the French and disrupt their plans. This gave Henry the initiative, for a while at least, as the French now had to track down the English army and find another suitable place to bring Henry to battle.

Having turned west at Miraumont, the English army moved on to lodge at the villages of Louvencourt, Acheux-en-Amiénois (Point 5) and Forceville on the night of 22 October. The family of Mailly, from the village of Mailly-Maillet on the route between Miraumont and Forceville, is said to have lost three members at Agincourt, including Charles VI de Mailly and his son. Acheux had underground refuges, created by early Christians and in use until the sixteenth century, which may have provided some safety for the villagers. It also had a castle dating from the eleventh century, with seven towers and a curtain wall surrounded by a dry ditch filled with thorn bushes, from which, according to local tradition, it derived its name of the Chateau des Épines, or castle of thorns.

Once beyond Péronne, the wide, open, flat plains characteristic of the area south of the Somme give way to more undulating terrain. The undulations become increasingly pronounced along the army's route, and there are several otherwise inconsequential streams or minor rivers nestling in valleys with marked slopes. The changes of elevation are not

The approach to the river Authie near Thièvres at the start of an increasingly steep descent into the river followed by a climb up onto the ridge beyond. (Peter Hoskins)

The river Authie between Thièvres and Doullens. This was not a major obstacle in its own right, but the challenges of crossing minor rivers were compounded by the steep valley sides. (Peter Hoskins)

A country road between Doullens and Bonnières. Moving carts and many thousands of horses and men along such roads would have been a significant challenge to Henry and his commanders. (Peter Hoskins)

great, but steeps descents into and climbs out of such valleys would have been tiring and challenging for carters in particular. The crossing of the Authie near Thièvres is a case in point, with the road descending steeply for 70m and then climbing equally steeply to a similar elevation on the other side. The difficulties would be compounded by poor roads which would rapidly deteriorate in rain and become churned up by the passage of horses and men.

On 23 October Henry set out from Acheux, crossing the river Authie at Thièvres, and passing between Lucheux (Point 8) and Doullens (Point 7). The army is reported to have passed through Beauquesne (Point 6). The town lies about 8km south of the river Authie so it is possible that foragers or scouts approached the town with the main body moving further north. Lucheux had a strong castle on the north side, built originally in the twelfth century; it was one of the most important fortresses in Picardy, in the ownership of the Count of St-Pol. The town itself was walled with a gate into the castle, and had suffered several English attacks during the earlier stages of the Hundred Years War. Doullens was fortified with crenellated walls, water-filled ditches, three gates and a castle. It was an important town, with two priories, an abbey and a female religious house, as well as several hospitals.

It is said locally that Henry came close to Doullens and his army lodged in the hamlets of Freschevillers, Hamencourt and la Vicogne just to the south-east of the town. However, the dates given are inaccurate, and Henry halted at Bonnières for the night of 23 October. Nevertheless, it is possible that Henry's army crossed the Authie at several places between Thièvres and Doullens and this could account for the reported English presence in the vicinity.

At Bonnières Henry was in a good position on high ground overlooking the valley of the river Canche. The men were billeted in numerous villages in the vicinity, but the Duke of York and the vanguard were sent 5km ahead of him to Frévent (Point 9), defended by a castle just to the north of the river, to secure the crossing of the river with a view to an unimpeded march north the next day. The duke achieved his objective, but not without difficulty since the bridge had been broken by the French and they had patrols in the area who attempted to disrupt the crossing. About 800m south-east of Frévent in the hamlet of Cercamp was a twelfth-century Cistercian monastery which is said to have been badly damaged and ransacked by the English troops.

The approach to the Ternoise at Blangy-sur-Ternoise. Maisoncelle and Agincourt lie beyond the ridge. (Peter Hoskins)

On 24 October Henry crossed the Canche and marched north. The Duke of York moved ahead with a portion of the vanguard. That this was a larger reconnaissance force than usual was dictated by the expectation that the French would seek battle that day. News indeed came that the French were assembling in strength ahead of Henry, although it may not yet have been clear precisely where. It was now imperative to cross the Ternoise, about 19km ahead, without delay.

The Ternoise now seems a minor river, but it lies in a flat valley about 800m wide which would probably have been marshy in the fifteenth century. With a steep climb of some 60m out of the valley onto higher ground, the army would have been vulnerable during the crossing of the river. However, the castle which had once stood at Blangy-sur-Ternoise to defend the crossing had long since been replaced by a Benedictine abbey. Furthermore, although the French had broken the bridge at Frévent and attempted to disrupt the crossing of the Canche, they do not seem to have destroyed the bridge at Blangy-sur-Ternoise (Point 10). There was some fighting during the day with several archers recorded as having been captured by the French and it is possible that these casualties were suffered as the French tried to hamper the English at the Ternoise. Nevertheless a successful crossing was made at Blangy-sur-Ternoise, and the army climbed out of the valley and moved forward 5km to Maisoncelle. At one point during the advance towards Blangy the king's herbergers had found him lodgings in a village. By the time the news reached Henry he had already passed the village, and he refused to turn back because he was wearing armour and he considered it inappropriate for him to be armed when dealing with civilians.

The river Ternoise at Blangy. (Peter Hoskins)

The approach to Maisoncelle and the battlefield beyond, having climbed out of the valley of the Ternoise. (Peter Hoskins)

Scouts brought Henry intelligence that the French were converging on the nearby villages of Agincourt and Ruisseauville, and as the English army emerged from the valley of the Ternoise and climbed onto the higher ground they saw the French army gathering ahead of them. Henry's men were only three days' march from Calais, but now the French were close at hand, astride the road to Calais and cutting off the road to safety. The main body of the army with Henry had had a long day's march of some 30km from Bonnières with crossings of the Canche and the Ternoise. They were no doubt tired. Perhaps some were dispirited by thoughts of a battle that was now inevitable, and might even follow that same day. An account of the battle, fought on Friday, 25 October, and a description of the battlefield are given in Tour 5.

The March to Calais

After Henry's great victory, the risk of significant French opposition during the onward march to Calais had diminished. However, many men from the French army had left the battle without fighting, and with the Duke of Brittany and his company still at large a French attack could not be ruled out and Henry had no wish to remain on the battlefield longer than was necessary. The English army returned to their lodgings at Maisoncelle after the battle, and set off for Calais the following day, 26 October. Henry probably arrived at Calais on 29 October, having lodged at Guînes (Point 13) the night before. The route from Maisoncelle to Guînes is unknown, but it is probable that the army took the most direct route, crossing the Aa at Fauquembergues (Point 11), the Bléquin at Nielles-lès-Bléquin (Point 12) and the Hem at Licques.

In addition to the residual risk of French attacks, Henry still faced the same problem as he had done earlier on the march: finding food for his army in a countryside where even today villages are few and far between along the route. The terrain ahead of them for the first two days until they descended into the coastal plain near Guînes was also much hillier than hitherto, with steeper climbs and descents. The recent heavy rain would have compounded their difficulties, and the onward march was still going to be demanding. But at least the safety of the Calais Pale was only two days away from Guînes.

Countryside north of Nielles-lès-Bléquin, typical of the route between Agincourt and Guînes. (Peter Hoskins)

If Henry marched more or less equal daily distances between Maisoncelle and Guînes, then a stop for the night of 26 October near Fauquembergues would be logical. The town, whose lord, John II de Beaumont, had died at the battle, was fortified with a castle and town walls with three gates. It had been damaged by an English expedition under Robert Knolles in 1370, and there had been a debate in 1405 concerning the need for repairs. Townsmen within the walls thought the defences should be restored, while those without thought that the fortified church and the castle, which were in good repair, should suffice. The matter was put to arbitration by the aldermen of St Omer who decided that all should contribute to repairs. How far these repairs had progressed ten years later is unknown, but Henry would in any case have had no interest in the town, save for any provisions that could be acquired, with his goal being a safe and expeditious journey to Calais with his high-ranking prisoners.

The next stop, on 27 October, would probably have been in and around the small villages about 10km south of Licques. On the following day the army would have passed close to the town, which does not appear to have been fortified but had a small fort, destroyed in the sixteenth century by Henry VIII, for its defence. By now it is likely that the news would have reached the town that a member of the family of the Lord of Licques, Guillaume d'Arroult, had died at the battle.

The final stop for the night before Henry's ceremonial entry into Calais was Guînes. The town had been in English hands in 1351 following the fall of Calais to Edward III in 1347, and only returned to French jurisdiction when Calais fell in 1558. In the fifteenth century Guînes was an important English town within the Calais Pale, and it had a substantial castle as part of the outlying defences of Calais, which also included a number of smaller fortresses. The coastal plain of the Pale was at sea level, with communications reliant on causeways across the marshland. Given the terrain, the fortifications and a typical garrison in time of war during the reign of Henry V of around 1,200 men, the Pale was well defended and the army could feel free of any residual threat as it descended to Guînes.

As Henry approached Calais to enter across the Nieulay bridge to the west, the captain of the town, accompanied by priests and clerks with the crosses and banners of the town's churches and all singing the Te Deum, came out to meet him. He was also well received by the townspeople as he entered the town. The men of the army were not so warmly received and had great difficulty finding food. Calais was difficult to provision at the best of times, so it was not surprising that the townspeople were reluctant to release their precious supplies. The

The descent to Guînes from the ridge 165m above the coastal plain of the Calais Pale. (Peter Hoskins)

difficulties that the men were experiencing were emphasized by reports of French prisoners being sold at well below the going rate simply so that the soldiers had money for food.

Henry does not seem to have been in any great hurry to leave personally, for three possible reasons: that he was waiting to ensure the safe departure of his men, that he was awaiting the French prisoners granted parole at Harfleur to report to Calais on Martinmas, 11 November, or that he was considering other operations to take fortresses, such as Ardres, surrounding the Calais Pale. In the event, it was decided that the recent victory 'should suffice for his honour at present', and, in view of the privations of his men, he arranged shipping to transport the army home as quickly as possible.

It is not clear precisely when Henry eventually left Calais, but it appears that he was back in England by 16 November. The great expedition had been brought to a close, but the administration of the army and accounting for the campaign continued. It was only in March 1417 that Henry finally drew a line under the accounts by agreeing with the Privy Council that those who had died at the battle should be paid to the end of the campaign in the same way as those who had survived. The final date was set as 24 November, eight days after the king's return to England.

The Route by Car

The Béthencourt Variant

This tour starts in Péronne (Point 1) and rejoins the route of Henry V's army after visiting the probable crossing point of the Somme near Béthencourt-sur-Somme (Point 2) and villages near which the army stopped for the night of 20 October 1415 (also covered in Tour 3). It finishes at Calais.

From Péronne, take the N17 to Éterpigny and then follow the D62 to Béthencourt-sur-Somme. The crossing point of the Somme was probably between this village and Voyennes. Turn left onto the D15 in Béthencourt-sur-Somme and the river comes into view shortly after crossing the canal bridge. Follow the D15 through Monchy-Lagache (Point 4) and turn left onto the D45. Follow the D45 and D937 through Athies (Point 3) to Péronne. Then follow the D938 towards Albert to join the main route.

The Main Route

To follow this tour without taking in the section between Béthencourt–sur-Somme and Péronne in Tour 3, leave Péronne on the D938 to Albert, and then take the D50 to Miraumont. From Miraumont follow the D107 to Puisieux, and turn left onto the D919 towards Amiens. At the intersection with the D938 at Hédauville turn right to Forceville, Acheux-en-Amiénois (Point 5), Louvencourt and on to Doullens (Point 7). The hamlets of Freschevillers and Hamencourt are on the D938 about 3.5km before reaching Doullens, and la Vicogne is just off to the right at Freschevillers. Thièvres, Henry's crossing point of the Authie, is a little over 1.5km off to the right from the D938 between Louvencourt and Doullens along the D1. Beauquesne (Point 6) is about 4km off to the left of the D938 and can be visited by following the D11 towards Amiens from Montplaisir, and then turning right on the D31. The main route at Doullens can be rejoined by following the D23 from Doullens and then the N25. Leave Doullens on the N25 towards Arras, and at the junction with the D5 turn left towards Lucheux (Point 8). From Lucheux follow the D127 to Bouquemaison and then the D916 through Frévent (Point 9) to Nuncq. Take the D104 to Blangy-sur-Ternoise (Point 10). Continue on the D104, and turn left onto the D107E2 to Maisoncelle. To visit Agincourt follow the D71E3. To complete the tour, leave Agincourt on the D71 and turn right on the D928 to

Fauquembergues (Point 11) and then take the D191 through Nielles-lès-Bléquin (Point 12) to Guînes (Point 13). For the last leg of the journey take the D127 to Calais (Point 14).

The Route on Foot and by Bike

This walking and cycling route is along a mixture of minor roads, tracks and footpaths. Initially the going is generally easy with few hills, but once beyond Péronne the undulations become more pronounced. From Agincourt until the coastal plain beyond Guînes the walking is over more hilly terrain with steeper climbs and descents and some steep paths. The distance covered on this tour is 178km. A variation of this route includes the likely crossing point of the Somme near Béthencourt-sur-Somme (Point 2), also covered at the end of Tour 3. This adds an additional 38km to the route.

The Béthencourt Variant

Leave Péronne (Point 1) on the D199. The road turns left through a right-angle after passing over a bridge, and after about a further 300m turns right through another right-angle. Take the second right in Flamicourt onto the Rue Roger Corne. Turn left into the Rue Jules Ferry and follow this road to Mesnil-Bruntel. On reaching the village turn left into the Chemin de Bas and after about 200m turn right onto an unnumbered road. Turn right onto the D88 and follow this road through Brie to St-Christ-Briost. Turn right onto the D45 and once across the river and the canal, turn left onto the D62 through Epenancourt and Pargny to Béthencourt-sur-Somme. Cross the canal on the D15, and from Villecourt follow unnumbered roads to Falvy. Turn right and follow the D103 to Athies (Point 3). Leave the village to the north following an unnumbered road, which initially runs just to the west of the D937, to Brie.

> *Part of the road from Athies to Brie is paved, but there are stretches with a surface of packed earth and stone. It is badly rutted in places and can be muddy in wet weather. An alternative for cyclists is to take the D937 from Athies and then turn left just after la Plaine Ferme to rejoin the route in Mesnil-Bruntel.*

From Brie retrace your steps to Péronne. Turn right onto the D88 and just before Mesnil-Bruntel turn left onto the unnumbered road taken on the way out from Péronne, identifiable by its no-entry sign for vehicles annotated *sauf riverains,* for about 300m. Turn right onto the Chemin de Bas and after about 200m turn left into the Rue du Jeu de Paume past Ferme de Brunte to Flamicourt on the outskirts of Péronne. In Flamicourt turn right and follow the Rue Roger Corne to join the D199 into Péronne.

> *An alternative route from Péronne to Béthencourt-sur-Somme is to leave Péronne on the N17 and then pick up the canal towpath. I have not used this route but the towpath is reputed to be passable on foot. Work is under way to upgrade the path and it may not be suitable for bicycles. Up-to-date information can be found on a local website: www.somme-nature.com/ nature/velo/vallee_de_la_somme_a_velo. The relevant route is Étape 1, from Ham to Péronne.*

The Main Route

Leave Péronne on the D938 through Cléry-sur-Somme and Maricourt until just beyond the junction with the D254. Turn left onto a track which rejoins the D938 near Bécordel-Bécourt after about 4km.

> *The track after the D938 junction with the D254 has a variety of surfaces; a small part is paved but most of it consists of packed stone and earth. There are also stretches where it is grass-covered. An alternative route for cyclists is to remain on the D938.*

Continue on the D938 through Albert, Forceville and Acheux-en-Amiénois (Point 5) to Louvencourt. After passing the church, the road turns left through a right-angle. Continue on the D938 for about 300m and then turn right onto an unnumbered road, forking left after about 150m. Continue on this track to join the *GR124* across the D124. Turn left onto the D152 and take the next turn on the right to follow an unnumbered road to Thièvres. The D938 is not generally busy but for long stretches it is straight and traffic moves rapidly. Particular caution needs to be exercised when walking on this road. Some respite from the D938 between Péronne and Albert can be found by taking roads through the villages to the north and south of the road, but at the cost of greater distances.

> *The route from Louvencourt via the GR124 is partly paved, but for much of its length the surface is packed earth and grass. An alternative route for cyclists is to remain on the D938 to Vauchelles-lès-Authie and then follow the D124 to Authie and the D176 to Thièvres.*

Take the D1 north out of Thièvres and just before leaving the village turn left onto an unnumbered road to Orville. Take the D24 to Amplier, and as the road swings left in the village continue on an unnumbered road towards Authieule. Continue through the village to Doullens (Point 7).

The map shows an unnumbered road leaving Doullens just to the east of the D916. After about 300m this road becomes a grass track that eventually peters out before reaching the D916. A scramble up a bank is required to reach the D916 and join the track which starts near a road-side cross. The D916 is busy, but following this road for a short distance from Doullens avoids the scramble up the bank. Follow the track north-west from the road-side cross, and after about 1km turn left at a crossroads onto an unnumbered road and then almost immediately right onto a track to Ransart. Continue on an unnumbered road and then a track to join the D196 into Barly.

> *Much of the walking route between Doullens and Barly is on natural surfaces, with stretches that are deeply rutted and very muddy in wet weather. An alternative route to Barly for cyclists is to leave Doullens on the D925 and turn right onto the D59 near Outrebois.*

Turn right to follow the D59 to Bonnières. From here follow the D114 and D916 to Frévent (Point 9). Continue on the D916, the Rue du Maréchal Leclerc, towards Nuncq. Shortly after the Ferme de la Garenne take the second unnumbered road to the left just on reaching some woods on the right. Follow this road across the D111 to Hautecôte and then take the D109 through Blangerval and Blangermont. About 700m beyond the church in Blangermont turn right onto an unnumbered road to Guinecourt. From Guinecourt follow the D105 to Œuf-en-Ternois. Continue on the D105 and about 1.1km after the junction with the D89 in Œuf-en-Ternois turn right onto an unnumbered road to rejoin the D105 just before Humières.

> *Part of the route between the D109 and Guinecourt is well paved but much of the surface is in poor condition. In addition, the section of the route from where it leaves the D105 beyond Œuf-en-Ternois until it rejoins this road just short of Humières is on a natural surface of packed earth and grass. It is rutted and muddy in wet weather. An alternative route for cyclists is to remain on the D109 from Blangermont to Linzeux, turn right onto the D101 and then left onto the D105 to rejoin the route at Humières.*

Continue on the D105 to Éclimeux. Take the D106 to Blangy-sur-Ternoise (Point 10), and turn left onto the D94. Turn right to follow the Rue de la Mairie and then the Rue du Moulin and cross the Route de Courcelles to join the *GRP Tour du Ternois Sud*. As the way-marked path swings left continue on the local walking path, the Sentier des Vallons, signposted and way-marked in yellow, which skirts the Bois de l'Abbaye. The map shows a break in the route at the north end of the woods between the footpath and an unnumbered road, but they are connected and the route can be followed without difficulty. Turn right at a T-junction on the outskirts of Maisoncelle to join the D107E2 and then take the D104 to Ruisseauville with the battlefield and the village of Agincourt on the left (see Tour 5 for a tour of the battlefield).

> *The walking route from Blangy-sur-Ternoise through the woods of the Bois de l'Abbaye is steep in parts and the natural surface is deeply rutted in places. An alternative route for cyclists is to take the D104 from Blangy to Ruisseauville.*

Continue on the D104 from Ruisseauville to join the D928 towards Fruges for about 400m and then turn left onto the D104 once more to Coupelle-Neuve. As the D104 turns right by the church continue straight ahead on the Rue du Marais. Continue north across the D130 to join the D343 to Coupelle-Vieille.

> *The northern half of the route from Coupelle-Neuve to the D130 is narrow and on a rutted, grass surface. Beyond the D130 the surface is packed earth and stone. Cyclists can avoid this part of the route by taking the D104 from Coupelle-Neuve, joining the D928 into Fruges and then the D343 to Coupelle-Vieille.*

Follow the D148 through Monteville. Approximately 600m after the junction with the D155E1 turn right and follow an unnumbered road across the D126 to join the D129E3 to Assonval. Leave Assonval on the *GR127A* footpath. After about 800m the path turns sharply left. Around 300m further on there is a sharp turn to the right. Leave the footpath and take the right-hand fork on a track to Renty.

The GR127A from Assonval climbs steeply on a grass and chalk surface which is slippery when wet. Steps have been cut into the side of the hill to aid walkers. From the top of the ridge the route follows a grass track, which is deeply rutted in places, until it joins a well paved unnumbered road about 600m before reaching Renty. An alternative route for cyclists is to take the D129E3 and D129 from Assonval to Renty.

Turn right onto a further unnumbered road on arriving at a T-junction in Renty. Cross the D928 at a roundabout and take an unnumbered road parallel to the D928 into Fauquembergues (Point 11). Take the D158 out of the town through St-Martin-d'Hardinghem to Williametz. Turn right onto an unnumbered road which climbs the ridge to the north. This road finishes after about 250m but a path continues in the same direction to join the D191 about 1km south-east of Cloquant. Continue on the D191 to cross the D341. About 750m after crossing the D341, at les Petites Madeleines, leave the D191 and take a narrow track for about 200m and follow the *GR127B* as far as a road-side cross in Vaudringhem. Continue straight ahead, following the footpath to the D203 and turn right to follow this road into Nielles-lès-Bléquin (Point 12).

The walking route beyond Williametz to the junction with the D191 is along a narrow path, which is steep initially, with a natural surface. The path between les Petites Madeleines and the D203 near Nielles-lès-Bléquin is steep in places and as far as Vaudringhem is on a packed stone surface which is badly rutted. The stretch beyond Vaudringhem is paved in some parts but some sections are made of packed stone and earth. An alternative route for cyclists is to follow the D191 from St-Martin-d'Hardinghem to Nielles-lès-Bléquin.

Leave Nielles-lès-Bléquin on the D191, but as the road swings sharply to the right just beyond the church carry straight on along an unnumbered road which turns to the west after about 50m. Follow this path past a roadside calvary mounted on a tree just as the path enters the woods, Grands Bois, and go up to the top of the ridge. Continue towards Monts Caboche and join the D204 into Quesques.

> *The section of the route from Nielles to Quesques from the roadside calvary to the top of the ridge, and again from the junction of the path with the unnumbered road near les Pâtis à Ruelles to about 550m short of Monts Caboche, is mainly on packed stone and earth, which is badly rutted in places. An alternative route for cyclists is to leave Nielles on the D191 and then take the D204 through Coulomby to Quesques.*

From Quesques rejoin the *GR127B* and follow this path until it turns sharply to the west about 1.5km north of Quesques. Leave the *GR127B* and continue on an unnumbered road across the D942/N42 to Escœuilles. Take the D215E3 to Surques and then follow the D215 through Licques to a crossroads to the west of Écottes. Turn left and follow the Rue de Dippendal to Bouquehault. Continue on this road, now the Rue de l'École, to the junction with the D248. Follow the D248 and then the D215 to Guînes (Point 13).

> *The section of the route from Écottes for about 500m is on a packed earth surface. This can be avoided by staying on the D215 from Écottes to Guînes.*

Leave Guînes initially on the D127 and then, as you approach the outskirts of the town, branch off to the right along the road to the east of the Canal de Calais à Guînes. This road eventually becomes a path, which continues to l'Écluse. The path is poorly maintained in parts, with a deeply rutted grass surface and bushes and trees encroaching into the path. Beyond les Marmousets to l'Écluse the path becomes impassable, and the unnumbered road alongside should be used.

> *Much of the section alongside the canal between Guînes and l'Écluse is unsuitable for cycling. The alternative route for cyclists is to follow the D127 from Guînes and rejoin the walking route at l'Écluse.*

From l'Écluse, turn right onto the D2471E1 and follow this road to Coulogne. Leave the village on the D247E4 to the junction with the D119. Turn left and follow this road into Calais (Point 14).

What to See

Péronne
Point 1: See Tour 3, Point 17, page 121.

Béthencourt-sur-Somme
Point 2: See Tour 3, Point 14, page 118.

Athies
Point 3: See Tour 3, Point 15, page 119.

Monchy-Lagache
Point 4: See Tour 3, Point 16, page 121.

Acheux-en-Amiénois
Point 5: The English lodged here and in the nearby villages of Louvencourt and Forceville on the night of 22 October. The eleventh-century Chateau des Épines was rebuilt in the seventeenth century but two of the earlier towers remain in the current building. The chateau is located behind the church, Rue Raymond Wazières (GPS 50.072098, 2.533394), but it is private property and not open to visitors. It is only visible if the gates to the drive are open.

Beauquesne
Point 6: English soldiers, probably scouts or foragers, were reported as having been at Beauquesne. The church of St Pierre with its thirteenth-century tower is in the Rue de l'Église and faces onto the Chaussée de Doullens (GPS 50.086563, 2.393527). The twelfth-century castle,

The church of St Pierre in Beauquesne showing the thirteenth-century tower. (Richard Kinnear) originally of quadrilateral form with ten towers and a large square keep, was demolished in the sixteenth century. It survives only in the name Ruelle du Vieux Chateau off the Rue Mathieu (GPS 50.082601, 2.390711), but the likely site of the castle was close to here in the south-west corner of the Place Publique (GPS 50.082446, 2.391488).

Doullens
Point 7: Henry's men are reported to have passed through three hamlets just to the south-east of Doullens: Hamencourt (GPS 50.141699, 2.357104), Freschevillers (GPS 50.139492, 2.363091) and la Vicogne (GPS 50.142373, 2.362908). In Doullens itself, which was bypassed by the English, of the many religious institutions present in the Middle Ages, only vestiges of the priory church of St Pierre (GPS 50.155428, 2.343382) remain in the Place Thélu.

The remains of the thirteenth-century church of St Pierre in Doullens. After many trials and tribulations across the ages it finally fell into disuse during the French Revolution. The nearby church of Notre Dame stands on the site of an earlier church of St Martin consecrated by Thomas Becket in 1170. (Peter Hoskins)

The Belfry, Lucheux. (Richard Kinnear)

Lucheux, church of St Léger. (Richard Kinnear)

Lucheux

Point 8: The English passed just to the south of Lucheux. The village has an exceptional collection of surviving medieval buildings. The parish church of St Léger in the Rue de l'Église (GPS 50.196181, 2.404987) dates in part from the twelfth century. The town belfry, in the Rue Jean Baptise Delecloy (GPS 50.197064, 2.411144), was built in the fourteenth century above an earlier town gate. There are substantial remains of the castle (GPS 50.198932, 2.409461) built in the twelfth, thirteenth and fourteenth centuries. In

The entrance to Lucheux Castle, one of the most important fortresses in Picardy. (Richard Kinnear)

November 1430 Joan of Arc was held briefly in the castle during her journey to her trial in Rouen. It is in private hands and is not open to visitors, but the entrance gate can be seen from the Rue du Chateau.

Frévent
Point 9: The Duke of York was sent forward by Henry to secure the crossing of the Canche at Frévent. In the fifteenth century a castle stood on high ground about 150m to the north of the river. Only the motte remains (GPS 50.280278, 2.291111). It is visible from a track leading off from the Place du Chateau. There are neither fences nor warning signs, but public access is reported to be forbidden for safety reasons.

The motte of the castle of Frévent. (Peter Hoskins)

Blangy-sur-Ternoise

Point 10: The English army crossed the Ternoise at Blangy-sur-Ternoise. The bridge over the river was possibly near the Benedictine abbey of Ste Berthe. There had been an abbey here since the ninth century, but the only surviving buildings are from the eighteenth century. The abbey is private property and is not open to visitors.

The abbey at Blangy-sur-Ternoise. (Peter Hoskins)

Fauquembergues

Point 11: Henry probably stopped in the vicinity of Fauquembergues for the first night after leaving Maisoncelle on the way to Calais. The church (GPS 50.600591, 2.098442) of St Léger, originally built in the thirteenth century, survives at the Place Abbé Delannoy, although it has been much modified over the centuries. An old postcard of the town indicates that there were, until at least the early twentieth century, surviving earth ramparts of the castle in the Rue de Fruges. The most likely location is between the Rue de Fruges and the cemetery (GPS 50.599297, 2.097722). Almost adjoining Fauquembergues is the village of St-Martin-d'Hardinghem, with a thirteenth-century church in the Rue de l'Église.

The church of Fauquembergues.
(Peter Hoskins)

The church of St-Martin-d'Hardinghem.
(Peter Hoskins)

The church of St Martin in Nielles-lès-Bléquin. (Peter Hoskins)

Nielles-lès-Bléquin

Point 12: The English army probably crossed the Bléquin at Nielles on the route between Maisoncelle and Calais. The church (GPS 50.675127, 2.030003) of St Martin can be found at the Impasse de l'Eglise. Much of it dates from the sixteenth century but the tower was built in the fourteenth century.

Guînes

Point 13: Guînes was Henry's last stop on the way to Calais. On his approach to the town Henry would have passed what would become The Field of Cloth of Gold (GPS 50.854753, 1.887453), the site of the meeting held close by the town in 1520 between Henry VIII and Francis I of France. In the fifteenth century the town had a strong castle. Only the motte on which the keep stood survives, now surmounted by a clock tower, in the Rue du Chateau (GPS 50.868446, 1.868811).

The motte of the castle in Guînes. (Peter Hoskins)

Calais

Point 14: Calais suffered extensive damage in the Second World War. However, the thirteenth-century watchtower, the Tour du Guet (GPS 50.958927, 1.849447), in the Place d'Armes and the church of Notre-Dame (GPS 50.958616, 1.853117) in the Rue Notre Dame survive from the Middle Ages. The town had been taken in 1347 after a siege lasting almost a year. It remained an English possession, and a valuable if expensive to maintain bridgehead for English monarchs, until 1558.

The thirteenth-century watch tower. (Peter Hoskins)

The church of Notre Dame in Calais was started in the thirteenth century. Further work was carried out during the English occupation, when it was within the diocese of Canterbury. (Peter Hoskins)

Rodin's sculpture of the Burghers of Calais. (Peter Hoskins)

In front of the Hôtel de Ville, just off the Boulevard Jacquard (GPS 50.952452, 1.853378) is a sculpture by Rodin commemorating the surrender of the town to Edward III by the burghers of Calais in 1347.

Maps

Maps at 1:25,000, 1:50,000 and 1:100,000 Scales		
Published by the *Institut National de l'Information Géographique et Forestière (IGN)* www.ign.fr		
Cartes de Randonnée – 1:25,000		
2508O – Péronne	2307O – Beauval	2205E – Fruges
2408O – Albert	2306O – St-Pol-sur-Ternoise	2204E – Lumbres
2407O – Acheux-en-Amiénois	2305O – Heuchin	2103ET – Calais
2307E – Doullens		
Série Orange – 1:50,000		
M2058 – Péronne	M2307 – Doullens	M2205 – Fruges
M2408 – Albert	M2306 – St-Pol-sur-Ternoise	M2204 – Desvres
M2407 – Bapaume	M2305 – Lillers	M2103 – Marquise
TOP 100 – 1:100,000		
TOP100103 – Amiens/Arras		TOP100101 – Lille/Boulogne-sur-Mer

How to Get There and Back by Public Transport

Beauvais, Lille and Paris airports are all practical for this tour. There is a shuttle bus service from Beauvais to the centre of Paris and there are good transport links from the Paris airports to the city centre. Lille airport has a shuttle bus service to the railway stations in the city. Péronne is within the Picardie *TER* region, but the final part of the service is provided by buses on which bicycles cannot be carried. For cyclists an alternative access to and from Péronne is by *TGV* to the TGV station Haute-Picardie 14km south-west of Péronne near Éstrées-Deniécourt. Calais is accessible by rail. Albert, within the *TER* Picardie region, is the only town along the route with rail access.

Where to Stay and Where to Eat
The websites listed below give information on local accommodation and restaurants for this tour:

www.picardietourisme.com
www.doullens-tourisme.com
www.ot-arras.fr
www.tourisme-7vallees.com
www.calais-cotedopale.com
www.tourisme-nordpasdecalais.fr
www.pas-de-calais.com

This tour is unusually well provided with places for refreshments at Péronne, Acheux-en-Amiénois, Doullens, Frévent, Blangy-sur-Ternoise, Agincourt, Quesques, Surques, Liques, Guînes, Coulogne, and Calais.

Tour Five
The Battlefield

Agincourt

This tour describes events from the arrival of Henry's army at Maisoncelle on the eve of battle and the battle itself on 25 October 1415. It also provides a guide to the generally accepted site of the battle between the villages of Agincourt and Tramecourt.

What Happened

The Eve of Battle – Thursday, 24 October 1415

Henry's army, having crossed the Ternoise at Blangy-sur-Ternoise and climbed 60m out of the river valley onto the gently undulating land beyond, moved towards the village of Maisoncelle. Scouts had located the French converging on the villages of Agincourt and Ruisseauville, 1.5km and 3km beyond Maisoncelle, and we are told that as the English reached the top of the hill they could see the gathering French army ahead of them. There are two exits from the valley of the Ternoise near Blangy that give access to the higher ground near Maisoncelle, one along the route of the modern D104, and the other along a track which skirts the western edge of the Bois de l'Abbaye. Both of these routes would bring the army up on to high ground with a view of the gathering French ahead of them.

Henry anticipated that the French might seek to fight that day and arrayed his own men for battle. What he may not have known was that although the French were already gathered in strength their army was still assembling and they were not yet ready to fight.

That the French were still assembling would be explained in part if the French summons to join battle, delivered to Henry by heralds on 20 October, was issued with Aubigny-en-Artois as the planned battlefield. Aubigny is about 40km east-south-east of Agincourt, and it seems from the route followed that Henry had initially set off towards the rendezvous. However, on 22 October he changed direction, away from Aubigny. Once the French became aware that Henry was moving away

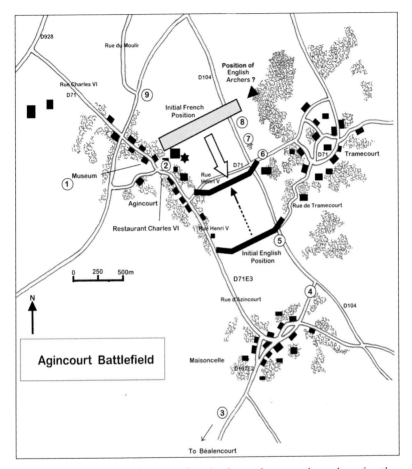

from the planned rendezvous they had to select another place for the battle, somewhere on Henry's line of march towards Calais. It had to be a field suitable for battle, but far enough from Calais that reinforcements could not sally forth from the English garrisons in the Calais Pale. Having selected the open ground near Agincourt and Ruisseauville they then needed to communicate the change of rendezvous to the companies of men either already en route to Aubigny or simply heading towards the general area of assembly. In the event, although sufficient forces had been assembled by 24 October to block Henry's march to Calais, some companies did not arrive until after the start of the battle and others did not arrive in time to contribute their strength.

As Henry and his men anticipated battle on 24 October, they took confession, consistent with the contemporary custom before combat. Henry also addressed his men. He encouraged them and said that he would rather die than be taken by the French with the burden of his ransom falling on the English people. It is also now, rather than earlier, either in the vicinity of Corbie or near Péronne, that he may have given orders for the archers to prepare stakes 1.8m long as a defence against cavalry. Some chroniclers report that the king rebuked Sir Walter Hungerford for wishing that there were 10,000 more archers present. This may or may not have occurred, but it was immortalized by Shakespeare in *Henry V* and has become a central part of the legend of Agincourt. It is not clear whether the French were also arrayed for battle, or if they simply assessed the size and disposition of the English. In any case Henry did not intend to be taken by surprise and kept his men in formation until sunset at around 5.00 p.m., when it became clear that the French would not attack that day. However, he was concerned that the French might encircle his army, and so repositioned his men to minimize this risk. The two armies then camped for the night, with the English centred on Maisoncelle, with Henry possibly lodged in a fortified manor owned by the abbey of St Georges in nearby Hesdin. The French were lodged to their north around Agincourt and Ruisseauville. Reports of their proximity vary from as little as 250 paces to around 800m, but the advanced posts of the two armies were certainly within hearing distance.

Henry V was alive to the risk of a surprise attack during the night, and in order that the normal clamour of camp life should not mask the noise of French movement he gave strict orders for silence throughout the English army. This order was to be enforced by harsh penalties: gentlemen would forfeit their horses and equipment, and archers and others of lower rank would have their right ear cut off. It was later reported by English writers that the French were so confident of victory that they placed guards to prevent any attempt by Henry to steal away, and that they also played dice to see who should take the king and the great nobles. It seems unlikely, however, that the English would have been able to infiltrate the French camp to gain such intelligence. More plausibly, it seems that Richemont may have been sent by the Duke of Orléans to approach the English encampment, but that after an exchange of bowshots the French withdrew to their camp. Similarly, it is reported that Henry sent some knights forward to reconnoitre the potential field of battle for the following day, although with the moon in its last quarter there would at best have been little light for the reconnaissance. If reports that it rained all night are true then reconnaissance of the battlefield would have been even more problematic in view of the lack of moonlight under the cloud cover.

No doubt those who could would have rested and slept as much as possible, but bows, armour and weapons would also have been prepared for the coming combat. It was reported that, despite the general order for silence in the English camp, trumpets and other instruments were sounded in the night to disconcert the French. The French had set up their camp in the fields between Agincourt and Tramecourt. Contrary to the English practice, where the king and the great lords took advantage of buildings for lodging, the French lords bivouacked in the fields while the men of lower rank found lodgings in the villages and nearby hamlets.

Accounts are varied and confusing, but there may have been negotiations between the French and English on the eve of battle. Some recount that Henry was prepared to offer up all that he had taken, including Harfleur, and to forgo ransoms due from captives and those on parole in return for a safe passage to Calais. It is suggested that there was a lively debate in the French camp. Some argued that despite their numerical advantage battle was always uncertain and it would be sensible to negotiate. Others argued that the English were poorly armed, foolish and away from home, and it was inferred that they could be easily defeated. Those who sought a negotiated settlement were accused of cowardice. There was also debate over whether or not it would be sensible to employ the communes, soldiers of lower rank, to confront the archers, since the men-at-arms were heavily armoured and would quickly get out of breath. Constable d'Albret and Marshal Boucicaut were of the former view, while the Dukes of Bourbon and Alençon argued that the French should certainly fight but that they had no need of the communes. Whatever the facts of the matter, it seems from these accounts that the lords present had sent word to the Dukes of Orléans and Brabant and the Count of Nevers, implying that not all of the French army had yet gathered. The decision not to fight on 24 October probably owes more to the incomplete state of the French army than any realistic prospect of the English being allowed to go peacefully on their way.

The English army was not going to increase in size, and the French had nothing to lose by waiting until companies en route to the rendezvous arrived. The original plan, when the intent had been to join the English in battle at the anticipated crossing of the Somme in the vicinity of Abbeville, had been for two main battles or divisions. The vanguard would be under the command of Constable d'Albret and Marshal Boucicaut, and the main battle under the command of the Duke of Alençon and the Count of Eu. There would be two wings of men on foot, under Richemont on the right and the Count of Vendôme and Guichard Dauphin on the left. In front of these two wings would be archers. A 1,000-strong squadron of cavalry under de Rambures would have the task of riding down the English archers, and a further squadron of 200 mounted men under de Bosredon would have the task of attacking the English baggage park. If the English were arrayed in a single battle then it was envisaged that the vanguard and the main battle would join up to fight as a single body.

At the meeting of the king's council at Rouen, a few days before the armies met near Agincourt, when it was decided that neither the king nor the dauphin would be at the impending battle, a revised plan was drawn up based on a larger army. It was also decided to overturn a previous decision not to include the Duke of Orléans in the French army. Now three battles were envisaged. The vanguard would include the Duke of Bourbon, Boucicaut and Guichard Dauphin. In the main battle would be the Dukes of Orléans, Alençon and Brittany, and d'Albret. In the rear-guard would be the Duke of Bar and the Counts of Nevers, Charolais and Vaudémont. The two wings would be led by Richemont and Tanneguy du Chastel. The body of the cavalry intended to break the English archers would be under either Clignet de Brabant or the Sire de Dampierre and the Seneschal of Hainault, John, Sire de Ligne. Of these, Brittany, Charolais and Tanneguy du Chastel were not present at the battle. The Count of Nevers probably arrived either late on 24 October or early on the day of battle. The Duke of Brabant arrived on 25 October after the battle had started. Thus, on 24 October, with some important lords absent from the army, there would have been a strong incentive for the French to delay battle.

The Duke of Brittany had been at Rouen for the meeting of the king's council on 20 October but by the day of battle was only at Amiens, some 110km from Rouen and 80km from the battlefield. It has been suggested that his absence from the battle was because he was dragging his feet due to his truce with Henry. However, it may simply have been because of either poor communications or lack of intelligence concerning the rendezvous point. At the time when the Duke of Orléans was asked not to join the French army, a similar request had been sent to the Duke of Burgundy. Although there was a change of heart concerning Orléans, it appears that the letter to Burgundy was never rescinded. Thus he was not present at the battle. A number of Burgundians were present, however, and the duke's son, the Count of Charolais, appears to have set out to join the army. However, for reasons that are unclear, it seems that the duke prevented Charolais from participating in the battle. Tanneguy du Chastel was *prévôt* of Paris and had stayed behind to defend the city, possibly to counter a perceived threat from the Duke of Burgundy.

The English and French Armies of the Hundred Years War
Raising and Maintaining Armies
Certain towns and castles would be garrisoned in times of peace, but in general the French and English kings did not maintain standing armies during the Hundred Years War. Instead, armies were raised for specific purposes or periods. The English armies were notable for the widespread use of the system of indenture for their recruitment and administration. Indentures were contracts between the king and his subordinate captains. They were so called because they were written in duplicate on a parchment that was then cut into two pieces along a toothed or indented line. In the case of any dispute, the two pieces could be matched to establish their authenticity. The indentures specified the size and composition of the company to be provided, with numbers of men-at-arms and archers. Pay, length and conditions of service, and terms for ransoms for prisoners and for the share of the spoils of war were also detailed.

In France at the start of the war armies were recruited through a feudal levy (the arrière-ban), but after the Battle of Poitiers in 1356 the system became discredited and Charles V introduced reforms. Armies during the French recovery from 1369 were composed of contracted volunteers commanded by captains appointed by the king, much as in the English case. They were well disciplined, centrally controlled and effective. By 1415 the political instability in France had undermined many of the reforms made by Charles V. Nevertheless, measures were put in place to raise taxes to fund troops supplied by the nobility and gentry, and royal officials such as the constable, marshal, admiral and master of the crossbowmen. During the latter stages of the Hundred Years War Charles VII prepared the way for an effective army to drive the English from France by re-establishing royal control of the army, designating commanders and providing the pay for the men.

Composition of the Armies
The English armies were generally home-grown, with men drawn from throughout England, Wales and Ireland. However, there were also sometimes contingents of Gascons drawn from the Duchy of Aquitaine, and soldiers of fortune from other areas are also found on muster rolls. Archers formed a substantial proportion of the men in English armies. The archers did not fight from horseback, but many were mounted for the march to increase their mobility. The ratio of archers to men-at-arms varied. At Crécy archers may have accounted for around half of the strength of the army, and at Poitiers they accounted for about one-third of the Black Prince's men. As the war progressed, the trend was for a larger proportion to be archers. The indentures for 1415 generally asked for three archers for every man-at-arms, but there were additional special archer companies from Cheshire, Lancashire and South Wales. At Agincourt the proportion of archers was around four-fifths. French armies made much greater use of mercenaries than the English, such as large numbers of specialist Genoese crossbowmen at Crécy, and they also drew on militia from the towns, as well as local levies of limited military value. There were also Scots men-at-arms in the French army at Poitiers and substantial numbers of Scots fighting alongside the French in the latter stages of the war, although not, it seems, at Agincourt. The French emphasis was on the man-at-arms rather than gens de trait (including both archers and crossbowmen).

Tactics
The preferred English tactic in set-piece battles was for the men-at-arms to dismount and fight on foot in a strong defensive position that optimized the effectiveness of the archers. The objective was to hold a position and wait for the enemy to come to them. This had worked well against the Scots

in the years before the Hundred Years War and at Crécy. At Poitiers the French did not initially oblige and it was only when the Black Prince was seen to be disengaging that the French launched an ill-coordinated attack. At Agincourt Henry V advanced towards the French to provoke a French attack, but then held his position as the French responded and moved forward to meet the English.

At Crécy the French had pinned their hopes on an attack by their mounted men-at-arms and knights, but the archers inflicted heavy casualties and the French finally broke on the line of dismounted English men-at-arms. However, French commanders were not slow to learn lessons from the impact of the archers at Crécy. At both Poitiers and Agincourt they adapted their tactics by fighting with the majority of their men on foot, with small squadrons of heavily armed cavalry used to attempt to neutralize the English archers. In both cases poor execution of the plan rendered these tactics ineffective and the main bodies of French men-at-arms were still exposed to the archers before they could come into hand-to-hand contact with the English.

The Day of Battle – Friday, 25 October 1415

The English army had been in France for the best part of three months and as a result had a strong sense of unity and mutual trust. Part of the French army had also been together for some time, shadowing the English as they made their way along the Somme. However, with many companies not arriving until the eve of battle, and indeed on the day of battle itself, the French lacked the cohesion of the English. This situation would have been exacerbated by the arrival of the Duke of Orléans as overall commander, probably on 24 October, bringing with him a change of plan which varied from that set out previously.

The numbers in the French army, and the formations in which they were arrayed, vary markedly in the various accounts of the battle. The size of the French army at the battle remains a matter of controversy, and many historians and writers consider that the French outnumbered the English several times over. However, the French king had issued orders in August to raise funds for an army of 6,000 men-at-arms and 3,000 archers, and the final figures seem not much greater than these, and thus closer to the numbers in the English army than is sometimes suggested. The vanguard is reported to have comprised 4,800 men-at-arms (3,000 with the constable and the marshal, 1,200 with the Duke of Bourbon, and 600 with the Duke of Orléans, commanded on his behalf by the Sire de Gaules). The second, or main battle, included 600 men with the Duke of Bar, and 1,200, 300, 400, 300 and 200 respectively with the Counts of Nevers, Eu, Marle, Vaudémont and Roucy and Braine. The Duke of Brabant, although arriving after the start of the battle, was also in this division with a small number of men, as were some barons from Hainault. Thus, the main battle had some 3,000 men. On the right wing was Richemont with the Viscount de Bellière and the Lord of Combourg and 600 men-at-arms. On the left were a similar number of men with the Count of Vendôme, Guichard Dauphin, and the Lords of Ivry, Hacqueville, Aumont and La Roche Guyon. There was also a further body of horsemen under Clignet de Brabant, although names and numbers are not clear. To these 9,000 men must be added archers, crossbowmen, some companies of militia from local towns and other men drawn in from the surrounding area to join in the defence of their lands and towns. Overall the French strength was probably around 12,000 men. A significant aspect of the French organization was the imbalance between the vanguard and the main battle, with considerably more men and most of the more senior commanders in the vanguard.

There is much more certainty about the strength of the English army. Henry had between 8,000 and 9,000 men. Thus, the numerical difference between the two armies was not large. What made the armies so very different was their composition. The French army was predominantly made up of men-at-arms, while Henry only had some 1,600 men-at-arms with the rest of his effective strength being archers. This discrepancy seems to have played a major role in the French planning, not least in their perception that their overwhelming superiority in men-at-arms and with cavalry earmarked to ride down the English archers they would have little difficulty in defeating Henry. Indeed, this probably explains why the vanguard's strength exceeded that of the main battle, with great lords vying for places in the front for what was, in their minds, likely to be a short, sharp encounter leading to an easy victory.

The deployment of the English army is not certain, but it is probable that the men-at-arms were divided into three battles, the vanguard under the Duke of York, the centre under the king and the rear-guard under the Lord Camoys. In view of the small numbers of men-at-arms, these divisions were most likely arrayed side by side across the battlefield. The deployment of the archers is also not entirely clear, but there were probably large contingents on each flank, deployed slightly in advance of the men-at-arms, with further smaller contingents between and in front of the three divisions of men-at-arms. There were also some 200 archers deployed forward, hidden in woods near Tramecourt close to the French rear-guard, whose role was to fire into the flanks of the French when they began to advance. The archers on the flanks would to some extent be hidden from view by the lie of the ground. They would also have been protected by the stakes driven into the ground with the intent of disrupting the French cavalry. It seems that the stakes were not arranged in a single line but in a more complex pattern that would make it harder for horses to pass through the defences.

The Longbow

The longbow used by archers in the armies of the English kings during the Hundred Years War was a formidable weapon. The bow was made of yew, imported ideally from the mountainous regions of Spain or Italy, about 1.8m long. The natural characteristics of the wood – the resistance to compression of the heart wood used inside the bow, and the resistance to tension of the sap wood used on the back of the bow – meant archers required great strength to draw the bow. Draw weights of 64kg may have been typical, with some thought to have been more than 80kg. For comparison, a modern sport longbow has a draw weight of between 13 and 27kg. Arrows typically weighed 113g, more than five times the weight of a modern competition arrow. Ranges of well in excess of 240m have been achieved with replica bows. One of the strengths of the longbow was its greater rate of shooting than that of the crossbow. It has been suggested that an archer could shoot up to twelve arrows per minute, compared to a crossbowman shooting two bolts per minute. One chronicler of the Battle of Crécy commented that the English archers could fire at three times the rate of a crossbowman, which suggests that a more realistic sustained rate of shooting might be closer to five or six arrows per minute. There is much debate over the effectiveness of the longbow. By the late fifteenth century high-quality plate armour provided increasingly effective protection against arrows, but few could afford such equipment and at the time of Agincourt armour was less well developed. That the longbow remained in service well into the sixteenth century, as witnessed by the finds on Henry

David Pim and Chris Dawson of the English Warbow Society with replica longbows of around 55kg and 50kg draw weight at full draw. (Peter Hoskins)

Steel armour-piercing arrow head. (Chris Dawson)

The medieval crossbow had a similar range to the longbow. However, its slow rate of shooting (two bolts per minute) made the crossbowman vulnerable and in need of protection by a shield or pavise. This illustration is of a replica crossbow from the end of the fourteenth/beginning of the fifteenth century, with a draw weight of around 70kg. (Frédéric Louessard)

VIII's *Mary Rose*, which sank in 1545, is testimony in itself to the effectiveness of the weapon. In addition, even where armour was not penetrated, the impact of just one arrow delivered with the force of such bows would have been considerable. Archers could shoot with considerable accuracy, and it was exceedingly dangerous for a man-at-arms to raise his visor. The future Henry V discovered this to his cost when he was shot in the face at the Battle of Shrewsbury in 1403.

The medieval crossbow had a long history, with progressive improvements made over the centuries. By the fourteenth century steel bows were in use, sometimes lashed to the stock with cord. Later bows had a range of mechanical aids for drawing the string, which allowed higher draw weights. In the early fifteenth century, however, three simple methods were predominant: placing the feet on the bow and pulling the string with the hands, placing the string in a hook on a waist belt and driving the bow away with a foot in a stirrup below the bow, and a similar system with two hooks for stronger bows. Earlier crossbows had a similar range to the longbow, but as stronger bows were made to take advantage of mechanical means of drawing the string, ranges increased to around 360m. The crossbow was an effective weapon. It had the advantage that it could be held in a cocked condition which enabled more deliberate aiming. However, its disadvantage compared to the longbow was its slow rate of shooting, around two bolts per minute. While drawing the bow the crossbowman was vulnerable and in need of protection by a shield or pavise. Its steel construction also made it a heavy weapon to hold and handle.

An artist's impression of a crossbowman with his pavise. (Paul Hitchen)

Beginnings

Sunrise on the day of battle would have been around 6.40 a.m., and since neither army could afford to be taken by surprise they were arrayed early in the morning. Henry is said to have heard mass three times, already dressed in his armour save for his helmet, and to have enquired as to the time as the army was drawn up. He was told that it was time for the service of Prime, typically held between 7.00 a.m. and 8.00 a.m. in winter. Henry is then said to have addressed his men, encouraging them to acquit themselves well for England and invoking the aid of God and St George. The king believed in the divine justice of his cause and the victory when it came would be attributed to the intervention of God in support of Henry.

It had been a standard tactic of English armies since the time of Henry's great-grandfather Edward III to fight on foot in a strong defensive position, and wait for the French to attack. With the French blocking the way to Calais, Henry was on the defensive and he initially adopted these Edwardian tactics and awaited the first move by the

French. However, much as had been the case with his great-uncle Edward the Black Prince at Poitiers in 1356, he could not wait indefinitely. The French numbers would be growing all the time, and Henry's army would, as time wore on, be subject to increasing problems in finding sufficient victuals. In addition, although drawing up his army had the advantage of minimizing the risk of being taken by surprise and allowed his men to focus on the task in hand, the longer they stood in position but inactive the more fragile their morale might become.

The French seem to have moved into position somewhat later than the English, which they could afford to do since the initiative lay with them. They are said to have been in position by the time of the service of Tierce, between 9.00 a.m. and 10.00 a.m. So by the time the French were arrayed, the English may already have been standing in their positions for perhaps as long as three hours. At some point before the battle, either on Thursday evening or on the Friday morning, negotiations are reported to have been held, aimed ostensibly at a peaceful settlement. Such negotiations were common in the period, and often were motivated by a sense of self-justification to demonstrate that all had been done to avoid the unnecessary spilling of Christian blood. It is unlikely that either side took them seriously on this occasion, but they served a useful purpose for the French, for whom delay was very much in their interest as they awaited the arrival of more contingents of men. The reported negotiating positions of the two sides were, in any case, irreconcilable in the circumstances. The French were prepared to allow Henry to proceed to Calais and to retain the town and the surrounding march-lands and Guienne, but he was to renounce his claim to the crown of France and surrender Harfleur. Henry's terms were similar to those his ambassadors had laid down in the spring: he wanted the Duchy of Guienne, five cities with links to the duchy, the County of Ponthieu and marriage to Catherine de Valois with a dowry of 800,000 *écus*.

The English took advantage of the delay to eat and drink. Scouts were sent out to check on the English flanks. To the left, behind the village of Agincourt, they found that there were no French present, and contented themselves by burning a house and a barn in the village belonging to the priory of St George in Hesdin. On the right they also found an absence of French troops, but located a suitable place to position archers in a meadow near Tramecourt close to the French rear-

An artist's impression of English archers. Archers wore a range of protection. If they were fortunate this could include mail, but more often than not they had to rely on some form of padded and reinforced jacket. Those who had protective headgear might wear steel helmets, including bascinets, or hats made of boiled leather over a wickerwork frame reinforced by steel strips. Archers would also carry weapons in addition to their bows, often a dagger, a sword or an axe. If they carried mallets for driving stakes into the ground, then these could also be used in close combat. (Paul Hitchen)

guard. Henry sent forward 200 archers to take advantage of this position. The French are also reported to have sent out mounted scouts, but they were driven off by archers.

There cannot be absolute certainty over the positions of the armies, but it is likely that the English were initially between the D71E and the D104, roughly aligned with the chateau and church of Tramecourt on the right where the Rue de Tramecourt joins the D104. The most noticeable feature of the terrain is the fall of the land away to the west, but looking back on the position from the advanced English position close to the D71, it is clear that Henry had chosen his position well to take advantage of a slight ridge running across the battlefield. The French at this stage were probably about 1km in front of them, just beyond Agincourt and well outside the range of the archers. In the fifteenth century woods on both sides of the battlefield came in closer than today. They would have provided some protection for the English from attacks on the flanks, and created a funnel narrowing towards the English position, giving Henry a strong defensive position.

First Moves

The time of the start of the battle is also uncertain, but it was unlikely to have been before 10.00 a.m., by which time the English would have been standing in their ranks for three hours or more. As the day wore on, the French advantage was steadily increasing as their numbers grew. Henry therefore elected to move his men forward. The king would have recognized that he was taking a risk. The challenge was to hold formation and also to have time to replant the stakes before the French could gather themselves and advance to contact with the English. It is possible that Henry moved forward around 500m and took up position more or less on the line of the D71 between Agincourt and Tramecourt, the modern Rue Henry V. He also ordered the baggage train to move up to the rear of the army from the overnight encampment. This may have been for a number of reasons: to reduce the vulnerability of the baggage train, to provide protection for the rear of the army should the French attempt to outflank the English, and also to bring the horses closer for quick access should a retreat be required. Whatever the motive, the redeployment of the baggage train had not been completed when the battle began.

It is at this point that Henry may have addressed his commanders to reinforce the rightness of his cause and to encourage them in the battle to come, and the order to advance would have been accompanied by a number of rituals. Soldiers would have knelt in prayer and taken a small piece of earth into their mouths, and the saints would have been invoked, probably by priests with the army. Banners were then raised to indicate both to Henry's army and to the French that combat was to begin. The order to move forward was signalled by Sir Thomas

A late fourteenth-century representation of St George and the Dragon in the Musée de la Guerre au Moyen Age, Castelnaud-la-Chapelle. The armour is typical of that worn by both sides at Agincourt, before complete sets of plate armour came into use. A bascinet with a visor is worn over a mail coiffe or cap with the mail also forming a gorget to protect the neck. Steel plate is worn on the chest, over mail and a padded jacket, and on the legs. The mail provides protection for the vulnerable armpits and groin not covered by plate armour. The saddle is made of wood covered in leather and sits high on the horse, giving the rider a stable position and lifting much of his weight away from the horse's spine. (Peter Hoskins)

Erpingham, mounted on horseback. The signal was given visually by Sir Thomas throwing a baton into the air. He is also reported to have shouted 'Nestroque!', which has sometimes been interpreted as an order for the archers to let loose, but since they were still well out of range at this stage the order may simply have been for the advance to begin. Sir Thomas then dismounted to join the king's battle, and as he did so the order to move forward would have been taken up with cries of 'Advance banners!' With a great shout and the sound of trumpets, the English moved forward.

The French appear to have been taken by surprise, presumably anticipating that the English would remain on the defensive and that the initiative for the start of combat rested with them. They were now compelled to respond, and as they did so it is likely that the 200 archers positioned near Tramecourt would have started shooting into the flanks of the French. At some point the main body of English archers would also have stopped, replanted their stakes and started shooting at the advancing men-at-arms. The effect of the archery, with more than 7,000 archers shooting at the advancing French, would have been very

An early fifteenth-century bascinet in the Musée de la Guerre au Moyen Age, Castelnaud-la-Chapelle, typical of the helmets worn by both French and English men-at-arms. (Peter Hoskins)

destructive. Whether the fire was continuous or in volleys is unknown, but in any case the impact on the French was considerable, killing and wounding men and disrupting their formation as they advanced. It was reported that the French initially advanced in line abreast, but then divided into three columns. This may have been to try to reduce the effect of the arrow fire, and secondly to concentrate force to break the English line. The momentum of the French advance on foot was diminished by the shooting of the archers, and the situation became worse the closer they came, as the English were now shooting at point-blank range from the front and the flanks. The French on the flanks were forced towards the centre by this shooting, and any attempt to maintain separate columns would probably have been futile. The lie of the land and the woods also funnelled the French into an ever-narrowing front, exacerbating their situation further. The effect of the shooting combined with the topography meant that the men in the very large vanguard were compressed into an unmanageable mass.

The French battle plan had envisaged the use of up to a thousand heavily armed and armoured cavalry to ride down and neutralize the archers. If the French had initiated the start of the battle, then the cavalry, setting off with the men-at-arms on foot, would have been in contact with the archers well before the men-at-arms closed with the

English. It seems that they did set off as the French men-at-arms moved off, but they had lost the initiative and their charge was probably not as well ordered as it might have been. The shooting of the archers was effective and horses stumbled, fell and wheeled about to escape the arrows. The horses who fell or turned hindered those who came after, and out-of-control cavalry disrupted the men-at-arms of the vanguard advancing on foot. Those of the cavalry who made it as far as the archers were confronted by the stakes, which further disrupted what was left of the cohesion of the charge and increased the vulnerability of the cavalry to point-blank shooting by the archers. The attempt to neutralize the archers with the cavalry charge failed, possibly in part because there were fewer mounted men than had been planned. These reduced numbers probably reflected the preference of the French nobility and gentry to engage in the *mêlée* against their English counterparts.

Crossbowmen and archers provided the French with a potential counter to the English archers, but they seem to have had little impact. They may have fired an initial ineffective volley, but it is more likely that they were positioned behind the men-at-arms and thus were never in a position to shoot effectively. A crossbow is armed by placing one foot in the stirrup and then drawing the bowstring. At the Battle of Crécy in 1346 the Genoese crossbowmen had found great difficulty in finding sufficient purchase to load their weapons, due to the slippery conditions with rain on chalky ground. It is possible that the crossbowmen at Agincourt faced similar difficulties because of the rain and mud.

At some stage while the battle was under way, probably during the early stages, there was an attack on the English baggage train by a group of some 200 men-at-arms supplemented by pages and servants. There is uncertainty about the leadership of the raid, but it may have been commanded by some local men: Isambard d'Azincourt, Robert de Bourneville and Rifart de Clamace. The objective was to distract the English and create fear of an attack on their rear. In the event the attack degenerated into little more than a search for booty, with the French falling on the tail of the baggage train as it moved forward to take up position behind the English army. Unfortunately for Henry, his baggage and bedding were among the items pillaged and his losses included a ceremonial sword and crown. A number of stories were told in the aftermath of the battle concerning Henry's losses. According to one tale the crown was taken to Paris to show that Henry had been defeated, but problems with timing make this no more than a story. The number of crowns also grew to two, according to some, one of which Henry intended to use for his coronation in Rheims, while the sword was said to be King Arthur's and so valuable that no one knew what to do with it. Some pack-horses were taken, but there were no recorded English casualties as a result of the attack. The raid had no impact on the course of the battle, and the only result was some personal inconvenience for the king and the loss of the horses.

The Clash of the Men-at-Arms
The archers had inflicted heavy losses on the French vanguard of men-at-arms on foot and on the cavalry, but they could not halt the oncoming French completely and at some point the men-at-arms of the two armies would clash in hand-to-hand combat. Before this could happen, the archers deployed in front of the English men-at-arms needed to disengage and move to the flanks to join the other archers behind their stakes. Since they were unencumbered by heavy armour and equipment, they would have been able to move relatively quickly.

Initially the English had been on firm, unploughed land, while the French were on soft ground sodden because of the heavy rain and newly sown with wheat. The English had moved forward onto this soft ground and now found that it was difficult to stand or advance. However, having advanced to precipitate the battle, the English could now hold their ground and wait for the French. For the French men-at-arms on foot the situation was far worse than for their English counterparts. They were advancing across muddy ground that had been churned up both by the initial charge of the cavalry and by the routed out-of-control horses. The sheer weight of numbers also worked to their disadvantage as those behind piled up on those in front. Furthermore they had to contend with the dead and the wounded obstructing their passage, and they were hampered by the need to keep their visors closed and their heads down in the face of the shooting which continued to come from the archers.

It is not clear whether or not the three English divisions were closed up into a single body or separate. In either case they were clearly identifiable from their banners, and the French divided into three columns to make for the standards and the centre of each battle. By the

An artist's impression of men-at-arms, showing the mix of mail and plate armour typical of the period before the general appearance of suits of plate armour in about 1420. Men-at-arms fought with lances, swords, axes, maces and battle hammers. At Agincourt the French, as they had at Poitiers, shortened their lances to make them easier to handle. The English did not do so, which gave them a significant advantage in the first contact with the French men-at-arms. (Paul Hitchen)

time the French made contact they were close to exhaustion. To add to their problems, they had shortened their lances to make them easier to handle in close combat, but the English had not done so and were able to thrust at the French and inflict wounds, particularly it seems to legs and groins, before they could strike at Henry's men. The French were

Ground near the English advanced position. This photograph was taken in October after two wet days following a prolonged dry spell. (Peter Hoskins)

also being funnelled together both by the nature of the battlefield and by those on the flanks moving inwards to try to avoid the arrows of the English archers. With the congestion, men not in the front rank crowded into those in front, and as men fell killed or wounded, others stumbled and fell. Bodies piled upon others, further hampering those who came on behind, who were so closely packed that they had great difficulty closing with the English and even raising their weapons. Nevertheless the combat was ferocious, and Henry was closely involved. He is said both to have stood over the wounded Duke of Gloucester to protect him and to have attempted to come to the aid of the Duke of York. Before he could do so, the Duke of Alençon had already killed him. The Duke of Alençon is then reported to have turned his attention to the king and struck him a blow to the head with an axe, which is said to have broken the crown on Henry's helmet. Seeing himself surrounded by the king's bodyguard, Alençon offered to yield but he was struck down and killed.

As the French became increasingly vulnerable, the archers joined in the hand-to-hand fighting from the flanks, encircling the men-at-arms as they crushed closer together. They used their own weapons and those taken from the fallen to deliver blows with axes, maces, pole-axes, mallets, hammers and stakes. Those of the French who had fallen wounded were also vulnerable to stabbing wounds through gaps between pieces of armour and through visors, and many of them suffered wounds to the neck and head. In addition, the archers continued to strike where breaks appeared in the French line, and the English men-at-arms exploited any gaps that appeared. The battle was going in favour of the English. When the French main battle was engaged, Henry drove forward into them with his own men-at-arms and further diminished the momentum of the French attack.

An artist's impression of Henry V with plate armour worn over mail. (Paul Hitchen)

The duration of the battle is uncertain, but we do know that the Duke of Brabant arrived close to the end. Since he had covered 48km that morning from Lens, he could not have arrived before 1.00 p.m. He arrived in haste ahead of most of his men and equipment. Seizing a banner from a trumpeter, he cut a hole in it for his head and wore it as a surcoat. He plunged straight into the fight but was immediately killed.

The Final Act

The defeat of the vanguard had been a great blow to the morale of the main battle. Not only was the defeat unexpected, but also the greater part of the leadership of the army had been killed or taken prisoner. Thus, although some at least of the second French battle had closed to engage the English, part of this division fled, along with whatever rear-guard remained. The battle was apparently won and the English could start to gather prisoners together, identify the dead and tend the wounded.

However, at some point Henry gave the order for the French prisoners to be killed. The reasons for the order, and its morality, have been the subject of debate over the centuries. It was a very unusual action; normally prisoners, certainly those of gentle birth who would have had a monetary value if ransomed, would be spared. Henry may have judged that able-bodied prisoners, perhaps in large numbers, at the rear of his army posed a significant threat, and it is probable that the order was given because he believed that the French were rallying, perhaps reinforced by those arriving late at the battlefield. This seems to be borne out by Ghillebert de Lannoy, who recalled later that when the Duke of Brabant arrived on the battlefield a shout went up that everyone should kill his prisoners. Lannoy had been among the prisoners but was one of those who survived, despite the English setting fire to the house in which he was held with ten or twelve other prisoners. Whatever the reason for it, many prisoners were killed. Nevertheless, some were not, and it is probable that the order was rescinded when the renewed threat did not materialize.

The Aftermath

Henry and his exhausted men had won the day, but much needed to be done before they could move on once more towards Calais. There are numerous, sometimes conflicting, accounts of the events that followed the battle, but it seems that the piles of bodies on the battlefield were searched by the English. They were looking for their own dead and wounded, but also removing coats of arms from the French dead to enable identification of those men of rank who had died. The English army also took armour and weapons from the dead. Henry ordered that men should not take more than they needed for their own personal use, and the rest was placed in a barn and burnt.

Henry kept the French away from the battlefield in the immediate aftermath, although they were allowed to come and collect their dead the next day. The battlefield was not guarded overnight and it seems that some French people came to remove bodies under cover of darkness. At some stage, probably after the departure of Henry's army, when the French returned to the battlefield, they found that a great deal of armour still remained. It also seems that there had been little looting of valuables by the English soldiery, but local peasants returned to strip the dead of remaining clothing, leaving them naked where they lay. At some stage the *bailli* of Amiens sent men to recover equipment left after the French defeat. He had to be content with just two cannon, two damaged *pavises* and parts of tents.

Casualties

Casualty figures cannot be established accurately, but the numbers of French dead seem to have been higher than at the defeats at Crécy (2,000–4,000) and Poitiers (around 2,500). Contemporary accounts vary markedly, and the best that can be said is that the French dead can be numbered in the thousands and the English in the hundreds. However, although the numbers of English killed and wounded overall were light, the Duke of York with the vanguard on the right of the English line suffered relatively heavy casualties, with the duke himself, and 90 of his company of 400 killed, although some of these may have been archers and not men-at-arms. Of the English dead, the bodies of the Duke of York and the Earl of Suffolk were boiled to strip the flesh from the bones, which were shipped home to England for burial. It is not entirely certain, but the bodies of the other English dead were probably burned.

For the French the stripping of the bodies led to great problems in identifying corpses. The Duke of Brabant, for example, was not identified until two days later, with the search for others continuing until the Wednesday after the battle. The French dead of rank who could be identified were taken away for burial, some nearby at Vieil Hesdin, but the leading peers were taken further afield. The other dead were said to have been buried in a number of pits on ground given by the Abbot of Ruisseauville near the calvary on the D104 and blessed on the orders of the Bishop of Thérouanne. Among the French dead of high rank were: the Archbishop of Sens; his nephew the Lord of Marcoussis; the Sires de Fauquembergues and Dampierre; the Counts of Nevers, Blâmont, Vaudémont and Roucy; the Dukes of Alençon, Bar and Brabant; and Constable d'Albret. The Azincourt family also suffered, with Jean, who was present at the battle despite being in the service of the absent Duke of Burgundy, and his son Regnault both killed.

Prisoners

As with casualty figures, there is some uncertainty over the numbers of French prisoners taken. One chronicler recorded a figure of 2,200, but the contemporary consensus was around 1,500. Some 282 can be identified by name, and among these were six men of considerable monetary and symbolic value: the Dukes of Orléans and Bourbon, the Counts of Eu, Vendôme and Richemont and Marshal Boucicaut.

Realizing this theoretical value was another matter, however, and the English crown did not in the event raise much money from ransoms.

The Battlefield by Car, on Foot or by Bike

The tour starts at the Centre Historique Médiéval and visits the nine recommended viewing points below. The total distance is just under 10km (8km on foot). Leave the museum on the D71 to Point 2. Continue on the D71E3 and D107E2 through Maisoncelle to Point 3. Retrace your steps on the D107E2 to the monument at Point 4 at the junction with the D104. Points 5, 6, 7 and 8 lie along the D104. To visit Point 9 stay on the D104 to Ruisseauville and take an unnumbered road through Happegarbe. This runs into the Rue du Moulin. Point 9 is on the sharp right turn in this road. Continue on the Rue du Moulin until you reach the D71. Turn left onto the D71 to return to the museum.

Walkers can shorten this tour by turning left onto a track as the D104 bends left towards Ruisseauville via Point 9 to the D71. The initial part of the track is a natural surface of stones and earth. The surface is in poor condition and in places can be muddy. An alternative for cyclists is to follow the motorist's route above.

What to See

The museum in Agincourt, Centre Historique Médiéval, is at 24 Rue Charles VI (GPS 50.463446, 2.127893), www.azincourt-medieval.fr, +33 (0)3 21 47 27 53. The museum has a range of displays of equipment and weapons, tells the history of the battle, and caters for group visits. It is open throughout the year from 10.00 a.m. to 5.00 p.m. from October to March, and from 10.00 a.m. to 6.00 p.m. from April to September. It is open every day of the week, but is closed on Tuesdays between November and March. There is car parking at the museum.

There is a restaurant, the Charles VI, at 12 Rue Charles VI (GPS 50.462299, 2.130414), www.restaurantcharles6.com, restaurantcharles6 @wanadoo.fr, telephone +33 (0)3 21 41 53 00, which serves snacks and meals. It may be closed outside advertised opening hours out of holiday seasons.

The Centre Historique Médiéval at Agincourt. (Peter Hoskins)

Site of the castle in Agincourt. (Peter Hoskins)

Points of Interest
Point 1: The tour starts from the Centre Historique Médiéval.

Point 2: The castle of Agincourt stood on the slightly higher ground opposite the church (GPS 50.462637, 2.129636). It was a modest affair with a single, 7m square, three-storey tower.

Point 3: About 300m from Maisoncelle on the D107E2 is a house with medieval cellars. The house replaced a fortified manor, present in 1415, with a single tower which would have afforded a good view of the gathering French army. The house is thought to have been used by Henry V for his lodgings on the eve of battle (GPS 50.405, 2.108333). It is private property and is not open to visitors. Opposite the house is the site of a chapel.

The site of the fortified manor where Henry V is believed to have stayed on the eve of battle. (Peter Hoskins)

Point 4: A monument to the battle, together with a map showing an interpretation of the action, lies at the junction of the D107E2 and the D104 near Tramecourt (GPS 50.45414, 2.15074). This is close to the probable English camp in Maisoncelle on the eve of battle. The English

The monument to those of both armies who fell at Agincourt. (Peter Hoskins)

The battlefield looking towards the French positions from the initial English deployment. It is not immediately obvious from here, but looking back from Point 6 Henry's chosen position can be seen to have taken advantage of a low ridge. (Peter Hoskins)

The final English position was probably near the D71. This view looks along the battlefield towards the French position. The calvary is on the right in the trees. Looking back from this road the ridge on which the army was initially arrayed can be seen distinctly. (Peter Hoskins)

translation of the somewhat flowery French on the information board gives the misleading impression that the mud was a more important factor in the battle than the shooting of the archers.

Point 5: The probable initial English position can be viewed from the junction of the Rue de Tramecourt and the D104 (GPS 50.45857, 2.145767).

Point 6: The D71 between the junction with the D71E3 and the D104 probably represents the line to which the English advanced, and where the men-at-arms of the two armies made contact (GPS 50.46249, 2.13757). Until the early twentieth century there was a wood, known as le Bois de Malheur, or Wood of Misfortune, which straddled the D104 just south of the crossroads between les Trente and la Gacogne. According to local tradition it was so called because it was here that the killing of the French prisoners took place.

Point 7: A calvary on the D104 about 180m to the north of the crossroads with the D71 (GPS 50.465174, 2.140376) is said to mark grave pits where around 6,000 of the French dead were buried. It was erected in 1870 by the Vicomte de Tramecourt, where excavations in 1818 were reported as revealing human remains. Grave pits containing several thousand dead are thought to lie between the calvary and the D71.

Point 8: About 300m further north-west along the D104 from the calvary is the probable position of the front rank of the French initial alignment (GPS 50.46753, 2.138686). The 200 archers deployed to fire into the flank of the French rear-guard may have been positioned a short distance further along the road towards Ruisseauville.

Point 9: The right-angled bend in the Rue du Moulin between Agincourt and Ruisseauville

The calvary. (Peter Hoskins)

(GPS 50.468787, 2.125962) is about 500m to the north-west of the front line of the French vanguard in their initial position before advancing towards the English army.

Maps

Maps at 1:25,000, 1:50,000 and 1:100,000 Scales
Published by the *Institut National de l'Information Géographique et Forestière (IGN)* www.ign.fr
Cartes de Randonnée – 1:25,000
2205E – Fruges
Série Orange – 1:50,000
M2205 – Fruges
TOP 100 – 1:100,000
TOP100101 – Lille/Boulogne-sur-Mer

How to Get There and Back by Public Transport

Beauvais, Lille and Paris airports are all practical for this tour. There is a shuttle bus service from Beauvais to the centre of Paris and there are good transport links from the Paris airports to the city centre. Lille airport has a shuttle bus service to the railway stations in the city. Hesdin, 15km distant, is the closest railway station to Agincourt. There is a bus service in school term time between Hesdin and Agincourt, which also runs through Maisoncelle and Blangy-sur-Ternoise, operated by Le Bus Colvert (Line 6429), www.pasdecalais.fr/les-bus-colvert.

Where to Stay and Where to Eat

The websites listed below give information on local accommodation and restaurants for this tour:

www.tourisme-7vallees.com
www.tourisme-nordpasdecalais.fr
www.pas-de-calais.com

FURTHER READING

There is a wide range of literature concerning the Battle of Agincourt and the Hundred Years War. The suggestions that follow are based largely on the author's personal preference, and cover the Agincourt campaign itself, the Hundred Years War in general, and the other great battles of the war that live in the English consciousness. Some useful websites are also listed.

Agincourt

Agincourt, a New History, Anne Curry (Stroud, 2005, pb edn 2006)

Agincourt 1415: Triumph Against the Odds, Matthew Bennett (Oxford, 1991)

Agincourt, the King, the Campaign, the Battle, Juliet Barker (London, 2005)

Azincourt, Bernard Cornwell (London, 2009) (an historical novel)

The Battle of Agincourt, Sources and Interpretations, Anne Curry, 2nd edn (Woodbridge, 2009)

1415: Henry V's Year of Glory, Ian Mortimer (London, 2010)

The Hundred Years War

The Hundred Years War, Anne Curry, 2nd edn (Basingstoke, 2003)

Trial by Battle, The Hundred Years War, Vol. 1, Jonathan Sumption (London, 1999)

Trial by Fire, The Hundred Years War, Vol. 2, Jonathan Sumption (London, 2001)

Divided Houses, The Hundred Years War, Vol. 3, Jonathan Sumption (London, 2012)

[Note: Volume 3 of Jonathan Sumption's books finishes at 1399. Further volumes are expected to complete the remaining years to 1453.]

The Agincourt War, Lt-Col. Alfred H. Burne (London, 1956; repr. Ware, 1999)

The Crécy War, Lt-Col. Alfred H. Burne (London, 1956; repr. Ware, 1999)

Crécy

The Battle of Crécy, 1346, Andrew Ayton and Sir Philip Preston (Woodbridge, 2007)

The Road to Crécy, The English Invasion of France, 1346, Morgen Witzel and Marilyn Livingstone (Edinburgh, 2005)

Poitiers

In the Steps of the Black Prince, the Road to Poitiers, 1355–1356, Peter Hoskins (Woodbridge, 2011; pb and Kindle edns Woodbridge, 2013)

The Battle of Poitiers, 1356, David Green (Stroud, 2002)

Armies

The Soldier in Later Medieval England, Adrian R. Bell, Anne Curry, Andy King and David Simkin (Oxford, 1913)

Agincourt 1415; Henry V, Sir Thomas Erpingham and the Triumph of the English Archers, ed. Anne Curry (Stroud, 2000)

Websites

The Soldier in Later Medieval England: www.medievalsoldier.org, an extensive, searchable database of those who served in English armies between 1369 and 1453.

The medieval centre and museum in Agincourt: www.azincourt-medieval.fr. The website includes teaching material to assist teachers leading school parties.

DVDs

Battlefield History TV, www.battlefieldhistory.tv have produced for Pen & Sword Digital a series of DVDs on the key battles of the Hundred Years War:

Crécy 1346

Poitiers 1356

Agincourt 1415

INDEX

Note: Since Henry V and Agincourt are mentioned frequently throughout the text, they are excluded from this index of people and places. Illustrations are indexed in bold type.